Copyright @2015

Preface

Good service is something you expect and something we all deserve. This book intends to share some basic fundamentals and provide insight to the reader on some of the how-to steps those in this industry need to take in order to thrive and prosper. Based on firsthand experience, the book offers examples and suggestions:

1. *on establishing unity of performance,*

2. *consistency of applied systems,*

3. *meaning of responsibility,*

4. *importance of organization, and*

5. *why admirable supervision and communication skills must lead the way.*

There is and will always be room for improvement in service in the quest for guest satisfaction.

The person in charge cannot allow complacency.

Not succumbing to the belief, "Don't push the river,

water will flow by itself."

We as service professionals must remain diligent

and remember we are in the happiness business:

Priding ourselves on the motto, "we aim to please."

In Loving Memory

For Jean, my wife and partner, my

inspiration

Acknowledgments

To my daughter Dottie

who had tirelessly invested time and effort to help publish this book.

To John A. Jordan,

one of a kind professional and gentlemen who inspired me to write this book.

To Mary Constantine,

valued friend and proofreader.

ABOUT THE AUTHOR

Phil Manos has been part of many gatherings and celebrations during his long and storied career of sixty-five years in the hospitality industry. Humbly said, he was front and center in guiding many stars of the entertainment world to the proverbial wall of fame. He was seen by many as the go-to-get-it-right guy from the back door of the kitchen to the adorned front entry facades. Phil never wavered in his belief that hard wok trumps the best mediocrity has to offer.

Mr. Manos served in the Army during the Korean Conflict. Beginning at the age of seventeen, he displayed his talents working at New York's Waldorf Astoria, The Stork Club, Delmonico's, the Copacabana, The Sea Pines Resort on Hilton Head Island, South Carolina, Shangri-La Resort in Oklahoma, Sands in Las Vegas, and Grossinger's Resort in the Catskills of New York.

Late in his career, he owned and managed two restaurants in the New York area. After spending eleven years at the Cherokee Town and Country Club in Atlanta, Georgia he retired and went on to form his own Food and Beverage Consulting Company.

A PERFECT AFFAIR is a book befitting a man who traded dishes on a tray to serve in words this wonderful how-to smorgasbord of his secrets to success.

TABLE OF CONTENTS

8

CHAPTER 1

SERVICE MANAGEMENT

This book is written for the Hospitality Industry's management and supervisory professionals. And to all those who follow who choose to enlist in their ranks.

Over sixty-five years working in multiple food and beverage operations in both management and consultant positions, I learned the hard way. Experience the best teacher and the best teacher experience. Successful operations for unique properties require an overall consistency in service, etiquette, and performance. Properly trained staff can achieve and project professionalism to its fullest potential. Skillful planning, organizing, executing, and performing all around excellence assures a quality experience for each guest. The ability to supervise effectively is key. Supervising one or more assistants, in turn means they will supervise others who hold different operational skills.

We are serving ladies and gentlemen, who in turn expect and rightfully demand, to be served by ladies and gentlemen – a most wonderful and rewarding combination. We are in the happiness business and our main purpose is to please (John Jordan). We are expected to provide two products: food and beverage. This requires us to be prepared and to serve professionally.

The most important factor we bear in responsibility, quality food and beverage service, requires a Chateaubriand receive the special attention it deserves. Accordingly, the hamburger needs to be served with equal respect. Why? Everyone believes that it is easy to cook and sell hamburgers with special trimmings and open a table service restaurant. Launching a new restaurant is a high risk investment. Four out of ten will go under the first year due to inexperience, poor management, and a shortage of revenue. Two out of ten establishments will survive. Success based on growth, reputation, and profit. Strong measurements must be instituted and executed in order to ensure that requirements in food safety, service, and employee appearance standards are met.

I served under and consulted with many top general managers who held administrative skills and sound general knowledge but lacked basic skills in the food and beverage arena.

For the benefit of young up-coming managers, whether fresh out of college or promoted from within, is to understand the importance of how the industry once was. The only fast food service restaurants were the White Castle restaurants in New York City along with other major cities. In New York the dining and nightclub competition among famous clubs and restaurants in a city of ten million people competed fiercely to attract the diner. Hollywood celebrities and wealthy patrons were offered the ultimate in food, service, and entertainment. A half hour before opening the dining room, the Maitre d' would line up service staff members who extended both hands out halfway for the Maitre d' to inspect for general appearance, nails, and clean handkerchief. Standard procedure for many establishments was a zero tolerance for lack of cleanliness.

The majority of the wait staff was hired for their foreign accent which added European flair to the setting.

Station captains were professionals trained in great detail by a master chef on how to cook specialty items at tableside. This training included learning how to cook with flair for the enjoyment of the party observing the preparation. This in turn attracted the attention of other guests – not only by exhibition, but the aromas created by the specialty items being prepared. Many restaurants would cook a garlic sauce just before opening to fill the dining room with an impressive aroma to stimulate the appetites of the arriving guests. In time, I have come to realize the great importance of experienced managers and supervisors in keeping up the tradition and reputation of the industry. Managerial persons must possess the ability and knowledge to train, and to supervise through constant observation while correcting and improving aspects of service and staff performance. Lack of proper training is analogous to sending a bunch of young boys out to play football without benefit of a coach.

Like coaching, success requires preparation. Professionally minded people do not choose this industry to win a popularity contest. They make a career that is honorable, respected, and which provides a decent and sometimes above average income. A person can obtain a stable position without a college degree or high school diploma. A wise man said: "Don't worry about training someone and losing them. Rather, worry about not training someone and have them stay."

Hiring new food and beverage personnel is a very important step. In reality we have no other alternative but to hire at random. Nine times out of ten we hire one person at a time, as fast as we can get them, and immediately throw that poor soul to the wolves by assigning them with someone to train because we are too busy to do it ourselves. That someone is generally not a skilled trainer. The employee acting as a trainer does not receive monetary compensation to train the newly hired which does not help – particularly if the assigned trainer is indifferent. This results in the blind leading the blind. Having good wait staff is a key ingredient in a successful recipe for a manager, supervisor, or department head.

Like most businesses, we should constantly be looking for good people to hire. Our livelihood depends on it. Slowly but surely we need to rid the bad apples and short-term employees. Until we find that special service crew. Instead of taking the time and effort to develop that ideal server, we too often take the easy way out. It is a big leap from someone good to someone who is great. Someone assigned to being a trainer is very important for the first few days to provide orientation for the newly hired person. In terms of getting acquainted with equipment locations, lockers, restrooms, meals, etc. From the time the employee reports for duty they are beholding to a supervisor in charge who will be the leader for that specific area; and will be responsible for all aspects of service. The fact that it takes longer to do the wrong thing requires the teacher to always be one step ahead so that all of the staff's efforts will be productive in saving both time and taking unnecessary steps. This is part of the learning curve. Culinary and management schools are essential in teaching management skills but they cannot teach the art of service unless they make a conscious effort to provide experienced how-to instruction.

Like any other business, if owners are not trained and prepared to manage effectively they will fail. They may survive for a while, but with challenges that lie ahead, unfortunately, the odds are not stacked in their favor for a lasting enterprise.

Only private clubs, hotels, established restaurants and dining rooms will survive for the simple reason revenue is generated from other sources; as well as having a captive audience of hotel guests or through membership dues.

In the private sector there are no extra funds or a captive audience. Only knowledge of operational skills, good tasting food, and impeccable service will keep the enterprise afloat and open for business.

Personal Note

On a personal note, this book is not written or intended to be the bible of what defines perfect service and performance, systems, areas of responsibilities, organization, and communication and supervision.

What is offered are suggestions whereby a system can be established that will produce results. Suggestions are based on years of extensive experience in many successful endeavors. If management is comfortable with its operation where little or few improvements are forthcoming; when managers and supervisors are managing or supervising only for the sake of their title, not focusing on how to improve service, they belong in the "don't push the river, it flows by itself" category.

All respected food service establishments institute and provide a level of service to its patrons. The good ones never forget there is always room for improvement.

Managers, Maitre d's and Team Leaders:

- You are professionals.
- You are the answer to a successful food and beverage operation.
- You are the force to provide motivation, observation, and supervision.
- You are the force to project authority and demand respect for decisions.
- You are the answer to ensure respect to this honorable profession.

- You and you alone are the answer to a successful operation.
- You make things happen.
- You are the answer to our industry's survival.

A. Personal Meetings

For any Food and Beverage operation to succeed means dealing with many people with different affiliations, personalities, abilities, and backgrounds. It is imperative managers get to know the people in their immediate area of responsibility. This is true whether one is a grill supervisor or head of a department. A manager should know the resume of a subordinate and establish a relationship with them. Trust, understanding, and a healthy connection between manager and their employee is imperative. Above all, establish respect for one another. Toward this end a manager should send a memo out to each individual requesting a meeting with them on a certain date in order to provide the opportunity to gather and share ideas. Ask if they have grievances or want to offer suggestions. Inquire about working conditions; have an open discussion regarding their work performance; where they excel, and where improvement may be needed. Ask if they need help in accomplishing goals. Tone of the meeting should be open and frank and looked upon as beneficial to both sides. It works.

MEMO EXAMPLE

Date:

_____

To: _____

From: _____

Re: Meeting

Please be advised of the following:

You are invited to attend a private meeting. Please arrange your schedule accordingly. Attendance is considered mandatory.

Thank you,

B. Service

At Cherokee Town and Country Club in Atlanta Georgia where I served as Food and Beverage Service Director for 11 years, members and guests were accustomed to receiving the ultimate in service by a professional wait staff. Consistency in execution, tempo, and cooperation was the expected norm. Operational importance centered on communication: from the highest level down to the Bus Person.

In service every item from a cocktail glass, glass of water, appetizer, main course, dessert, and cup of coffee has a purpose, shape, character, and position of its own. On every table each item must be properly handled, presented, and positioned from placement to removal by avoiding sacrificing service for the sake of speed. I do agree that speed and quickness is necessary for many reasons but not to the degree where it is obviously counterproductive to move too fast.

C. Food and Beverage Classes

Food and beverage training classes should be conducted at least two to three times annually for the benefit of new and regular service staff members.

The classes should be mandatory for all service staff and should last for an hour and a half. Preferably the best times are between 8:30 A.M. and 10:00 A.M.; 3:00 P.M. and 4:30 P.M. Each attendee will receive the minimum hourly wage with special attention to avoid overtime pay.

The classes are beneficial in that they ensure that service is kept uniform, consistent, efficient, and in accordance with service etiquette.

D. Consistency

Consistency is one of the areas where realizing the best service cannot be performed without it. This is true whether it be a dinner for two in a dining room or for a party of three hundred in a banquet hall.

Next to what it means to service guests correctly, consistency is the follow through. All servers should be performing as one-in the same way.

There is no reason management and service trainers should neglect or cut corners for the sake of speed of training. This area is one of the major areas in which service is based.

Classes, supervised performance, and meetings before and after a shift are necessary to remind and impress upon servers how service is to be performed and how it was performed.

E. Appearance and Hygiene

Appearance and personal hygiene are frequently the most common weaknesses for servers. Both are on top of the list of requirements for their profession. Not enough can be said or written to convince people to change personal habits, their appearance, and hygiene in general. One can easily spot an applicant who isn't groomed, not dressed properly, or perhaps seen chewing on a toothpick or stick of gum.

This particular area must be strongly enforced as standard procedure for all service employees. When entering the specific area of assignment reporting for duty, the supervisor in charge must make a timely and visual inspection and approve the server's appearance. And to take note of the time the server begins their shift. If the server's appearance and hygiene a supervisor does not approve of, a warning or penalty can be levied. In order to assist the employee, it is strongly recommended that a full length mirror be installed on the inside of the locker room door so that a server can check their appearance before reporting for duty knowing that they will be subjected to an inspection.

Place a sign above the mirror: **WHAT YOU SEE IS WHAT THEY SEE**! The net effect will include letters of praise from customers complimenting the staff's appearance.

HAIR, its length and style, is a trademark of a person. But it can be a big problem for a fine establishment to demand a certain style in today's world of fashion. Hair that is too long; straight hair for women with long hair; and an array of facial designs for men which feature hair constantly hanging over their eyes and face may be stylish but are unacceptable for any establishment.

Above all else, servers must not touch their hair, or the hair of anyone else, at any time when serving food.

Below are personal hygiene and appearance descriptions which must be handled discretely for each server.

Women	Men
Ponytail	Clean shaven (no 5 o'clock shadow)
Bun	Trimmed moustache (no beard)
Braids over the shoulder	Long hair above the shoulder
Boy-cut	No greasy, unflattering hair
Shoulder length	No nose hair
Not too much makeup or not properly applied	No ponytails
No unflattering hair style	Clean and trimmed fingernails
No rubber bands showing in hair	Spotless cuff
No gum or candy chewing	Tie straight attached to shirt (not loose)
No nails that are not trimmed and well polished	No beards (management call)
No rings on every finger other than class, engagement, wedding, or friendship rings	No rings on every finger other than class, engagement, wedding, or friendship rings

No lapel pins or ribbons other than name plate

No necklaces of any kind are acceptable

No earrings bigger than an American quarter

No sunglasses

No loose bracelets other than a watch

No visible bra strap

No clinging or extra tight slacks or skirts

No skirts above the knee

No lapel pins or ribbons other than name plate

No hanging necklaces

No earrings of any kind

No sunglasses

No pants below the shoe rim

No combs or brushes sticking out of pocket

A neat and clean appearance will reflect immediately a person's identity; a desire to be attractive to others; so little can say so much about an individual. Appearance and people's expectations of staff are crucial. The establishment's reputation is on the line. First impression a customer will make. One never gets a second chance to correct that impression. Next to appearance, hygiene is the other area on the top of the list. There is no other experience I can think of that is worse for a diner than come into contact with a server with offensive body odor, bad breath, or smokers breath.

These offenses will destroy a diner's appetite and reflect on the server, management, and creates a lasting stigma.

Servers are always next to, nearby, or passing a diner. Servers walk between tables, take orders, serve and clear, pour water and coffee or are always reaching for an item. Bluntly put, a server's armpit is often juxtaposed next to a diner's nose. The diner is going to eat food served by that person. It is well known that many servers have body odor and a bad breath problem. Both these conditions occur naturally or can be a result of a medical condition. In either case, such conditions must be monitored to ensure the effect they have remains on the radar screen for scrutiny.

BAD BREATH can be disguised with mouth spray used before entering for duty. Munching on a small piece of lemon or orange peel, a few leaves of parsley, or a cocktail olive will help as well.

BODY ODOR is helped by using powder and deodorant when changing into a uniform. Always wear clean, washable inner and outer garments or another clean uniform. Do not wear a uniform for more than two consecutive days. Avoid use of strong perfumes or colognes. Issued uniforms represent the face of the establishment. If the uniform is dirty, wrinkled, and spotted with grease, it will be noticed by the diner right away.

Uniforms:

1. Clean white shirt or blouse.
2. Shined, clean, and comfortable shoes. No loafers, boots, or scruffy looking shoes.

3. Black socks for men. Skin colored pantyhose or stockings for women.
4. Not black pantyhose unless it coincides with the color of the uniform.
5. No runs in stockings.

Supervisors must approach a deficiency in dress problem in private without creating hostility or embarrassment to the server involved.

PERFUMES-COLOGNES can be unpleasant, annoying, and offensive to customers. A cause for alarm management needs to be concerned about. A strong perfume or cologne worn by passing wait staff can affect an entire dining room. Applying such cosmetics just before entering the room might well soil items when setting tables, touching glasses, presenting menus and most importantly touching plates of food and silverware.

Appearance and hygiene must fit the style and expectations the club or restaurant decides it wants to project.

G. Entering Private Club Property

All member areas must be respected by staff when entering or leaving the club's private property. Staff may pass, and meet or greet a member. Wearing of proper attire must be adhered to at all times. This means:

No cut-off's

No torn jeans or pants

No going shirtless

No shirts with offensive logos – x-rated, improper language, race or religious defamation

All staff employees should be informed and reminded of these requirements during the hiring processes and at regular staff meetings.

H. Fancy Equipment and Service

Many private clubs, name hotels and top restaurants can afford expensive all silver set platters, base plates, and silverware, will show off, if you will, the class and reputation of the establishment.

Silver items and décor are expensive commodities and are expected by patrons willing to pay to be part of the experience. If the service is mediocre and the silver isn't polished a first impression turns bad very quickly.

China platters suddenly look just as classy as silver ones if the service is professional. Service is the absolute expectation for a host who is with family, friends or business associates.

Good food and outstanding service ensures the host never has to apologize for a bad experience.

In private clubs a member experiencing bad food and/or service will bring it immediately to management's attention. In the public sector, there will be a loss of a customer who has no invested interest in explaining his/her disappointment. Damage is done. And it's permanent.

CHAPTER 2

HOW TO DEVELOP A GREAT SERVER

A. Meetings

Short classes and meetings are essential and are to be held one half hour prior to main dining room, banquet, or other functions' opening for operation. It should be standard daily procedure before any function; to pave the way for a smooth operation. It eliminates confusion by providing instructions for servers and what is expected of them. This keeps the service staff on their toes by establishing that you are the leader to follow. Form an open forum meeting based on trust and understanding between management and staff. Talk about last night's performance. If something went wrong, use meetings as mini-training sessions. Find solutions together, ask for ideas and give praise for a job well done. Seek to keep their jobs interesting and exciting. Talk about tonight's business: how many reservations are expected, VIP's, birthdays, anniversaries, and members or persons asked to be served by "Bill" and "George." Invite the chef to participate to explain new items, specials, preparation and presentation. Ask the chef for his input on the service staffs' performance the night before. Ask the staff to inform the chef regarding the kitchen's performance relative to compliments, comments, complaints, slow production, cold food or food not properly prepared. It is also important for the chef to educate the service staff with a written explanation of the four mother sauces and their ingredients in the event a person is allergic to certain herbs or spices. Doing so will avoid the server having to go to the kitchen to inquire.

Have the sommelier or wine steward teach the server about the proper wines to complement the choice of food and cooking methods. With the talent and creativity of the chef, many varieties of sauces can be made based on the mother sauces. Use a little reverse psychology to keep one step ahead of the staff. Focus on what a person can do and not on what they know. We cannot change personalities or teach talent and we must not overload servers beyond their limits.

Let them know who you are and where you are coming from. Use diplomacy to deal with staff. Don't be tyrannical. Compliment your staff as often as possible but also privately reprimand when necessary.

Have a personal meeting with each one of your staff by asking if they are happy or unhappy at work and how you may help them. Reward an individual staff member for effort and performance by promotion, extra guest seating, etc.

This book is not intended to tell or remind you that the fork goes to the left and the knife to the right or that we serve from the left and clear from the right. It is written to assist you in experiencing standard procedures and to point out many important factors required in providing proper service. Quality of service is something we as managers and supervisors have the tendency to overlook because of our own personal and job related problems. And yes, sometimes admittedly, even due to lack of interest.

Lack of interest (get yourself another job).

Work overload (Don't bite off more than you can chew).

Knowledge to train (learn how or find someone who can).

Communications when service standards are communicated but not enforced, proper service becomes a 3-ring circus).

In-house politics (will eventually result in unfriendliness, bad working conditions, loss of interest and self-respect).

We deal with all people whether they are staff or a member/customer. People by nature bring their problems to work or to the dining room table. Dealing with problematic people requires control, diplomacy and calmness. It is said that the member/customer is always right but the customer arriving consumed by a personal problem requires calmness and the proper way to respond.

B. **Uniform**

Uniforms are very expensive to purchase, wash, and dry clean. Employees who are issued a uniform should be responsible to maintain and return it when they leave. Establishments can protect themselves by having an employee sign and agree to the uniform being returned. As part of the uniform's cost, a deposit should be required. The deposit will be deducted from the paycheck at intervals of a given sum per week. Such a system protects the establishment's investment as well as ensuring that the employee receives the deposit in return for returning their issued uniform

UNIFORM ISSUE CARD

Employee Name: _____   Department: _____

Position: _____   Hire Date: _____

Type of Uniform: _____   Cost of Uniform: _____

Issue Date: _____   Return Date: _____

I understand the above uniform is provided for the performance of my job. It is my responsibility to provide proper care and maintenance of this uniform. A deposit of $_____ for the uniform will be deducted from my pay in intervals of $_____ per week, and will be refunded if the uniform is returned in useable condition, free of rips, tears, or stains.

Normal wear of the uniform is expected and what is acceptable or not will be determined by my department head. I agree that ESTABISMENT will hold my separation check until said uniform or uniforms have been returned to my department head

Total Deposit: _____   Rate of Deduction: $_____ per week.

Print Name: _____

Employee Signature: _____

Date: _____

Uniform has been returned in usable condition and the above deposit may be refunded.

Print Name: _____

Manager Signature: _____

Date: _____

Employee has returned uniform soiled and/or failed to return uniform (do not refund deposit).

Print Name: _____

Manager Signature: _____

Date: _____

CHAPTER 3

DINING ROOM PREPARATION

A. Bus Person

Before opening, the dining room service areas must be fully stocked by the bus persons or by the service staff in rotation with all the necessary standard items and condiments. This is known as the "drug store."

A bus person is every bit as important as a server for the duties required to be performed and to be responsible for keeping the service area clean and fully stocked. Always clear tables with a tray lined with a napkin on a tray jack and remove used items in the same way with which they were served. No bus boxes should be used for clearing a table. Do not pick up glasses more than one at a time. Always keep hands and fingers as far away as possible from the lip of the glass. When loading the tray, place heavy items in the center of the tray. But do not scrape leftover food into one plate to save room. Handle utensils from the handle only and handle glasses from the middle placing them on one side of the tray. For re-setting it is imperative to know the proper table setting of the establishment as to what other than a lamp is to be a part of the re-setting. No other items but the salt and pepper shakers should be part of the re-set with the salt shaker placed to the right of the pepper and facing the entrance in the middle of the table. This provides a uniformed dining room setting. Sugar, cream, and sweeteners are to be delivered only when coffee or tea is requested. If not, place with beverages after a dessert order has been taken. All other items are to be carried on a napkin lined tray along with a tray jack (if oval service tray) and always placed properly with a napkin in hand. The chairs need to be placed just touching the table cloth which clean and free of crumbs. Usable items are to be returned to the kitchen. The bus person is an apprentice for a server and should be assisting servers in serving if time allows. This allows the bus person to learn how to be led in order to lead in the dining experience. It establishes and builds rapport for a long term team relationship.

A. Table Setting Requirements

1. All tables are in perfect alignment.
2. The tablecloth is even on all sides with the hem down.
3. The base plates are one inch from the rim of the table and free of fingerprints.
4. Napkin folds are uniform (type of fold a preference) and placed above the house logo, if any.
5. Handle tableware with napkins from a lined tray by holding pieces from the sides and placing one inch from the rim in line with the base plate.
6. Salt and pepper shakers are full and placed at the same place on each table with the salt to the right.
7. A clean vase and fresh flower, if any.
8. A clean lamp with full candle.
9. Chairs free of crumbs are just touching the tablecloth.
   Water glasses are inspected for cleanliness. In addition, add a white wine glass next to the water glass to entice one to order wine (optional).
10. Do not preset sugars or creamers. They should be brought in with the coffee and tea.
11. Place reserved cards in the same place on each table facing the entrance.

Proper Silverware Pre-Setups

1. Two dinner knives and teaspoon to the right.
2. One dinner and one salad fork to the left.
3. Place silverware one inch from the rim of the table and one inch from the rim of the base plate on both sides.
4. Place water glass one inch above the tip of first knife.
5. Placed butter plate two inches above and to the left of the salad fork's tip and the butter knife on the right side of the butter plate just above the salad fork.
6. Choice of napkin fold is placed above establishment's logo, if any, on the base plate.

After an order is taken, place the proper utensils at this time, i.e. fish fork and knife for seafood, steak knives for meats, oyster fork, or soup spoon. Have a pepper mill ready for use for each course. The dining room station is the sole responsibility of a server or a team of servers to set according to specifications for each function or per a standard setup for breakfast, lunch or dinner.

1. No base plates are required for lunch.
2. Base plates are required for dinner functions.
3. Pre-set coffee cups are acceptable for luncheons.
4. No white glove service is required for luncheons unless requested.
5. Pre-set appetizers are acceptable for luncheons and only for dinner if requested.
6. If formal dress is required for banquet dinner, white glove service is the choice for such an event.

7. White gloves are required passing hors d'oeuvres before a banquet party whether requested or not.
8. For bridal dinners all tables should be skirted – bride's table, cake table, groom's cake table, bride's book table and gift table.

B. Reserved Tables

Reservation cards are very important. Cards should be marked in bold black letters and placed facing the entrance in full view for approaching persons to easily see. For private clubs, write the member's club number on the inside of the card. The card should not be removed until the server and/or cocktail person greets the host by name and thus is able to read the membership number without having to ask for the number in front of the host's guests.

The same applies to restaurants whenever reservations are required. When the Maitre d' or hostess is escorting a party, all available staff members are to volunteer assisting in pulling a chair and to issue greeting. To a private club member (other than those outside playing golf and tennis) the dining room is the apple of their eye, their pride and joy, mirror to their ego, their home away from home. The place they are known, called by name, and served by their favorite server; it is the ideal place to brag about themselves and conduct business with friends and associates.

CHAPTER 4

RESERVATIONS SYSTEMS

A. Service by a Single Server
vs.
Service by a Team of Servers

Develop an effective team by design. The most productive system for best service practice for member diner satisfaction is to establish a station assigned to a team of servers which consists of one captain and one runner. Working in teams will allow for constant floor coverage by the captain and a steady tempo of food delivery from the runner. A team of experienced servers can rotate positions on weekly or monthly intervals if desired. Two servers working together for the same purpose will assist and help one another to meet the stations' demands. The captain stays on the floor constantly to be available to present menus and to take orders or to deal with any request by the diner. This sets the tempo of service for serving and clearing. The runner receives the orders and immediately turns them in to production for timely preparation and delivery. When time is available, the team can serve a party of four simultaneously. A single server who is responsible for a number of tables will be "in the weeds" almost from the very start on a busy night and unavailable most of the time to ensure a smooth tempo of service. With team work, nothing is left to chance and compliments will flow freely.

Dining Room Set Up

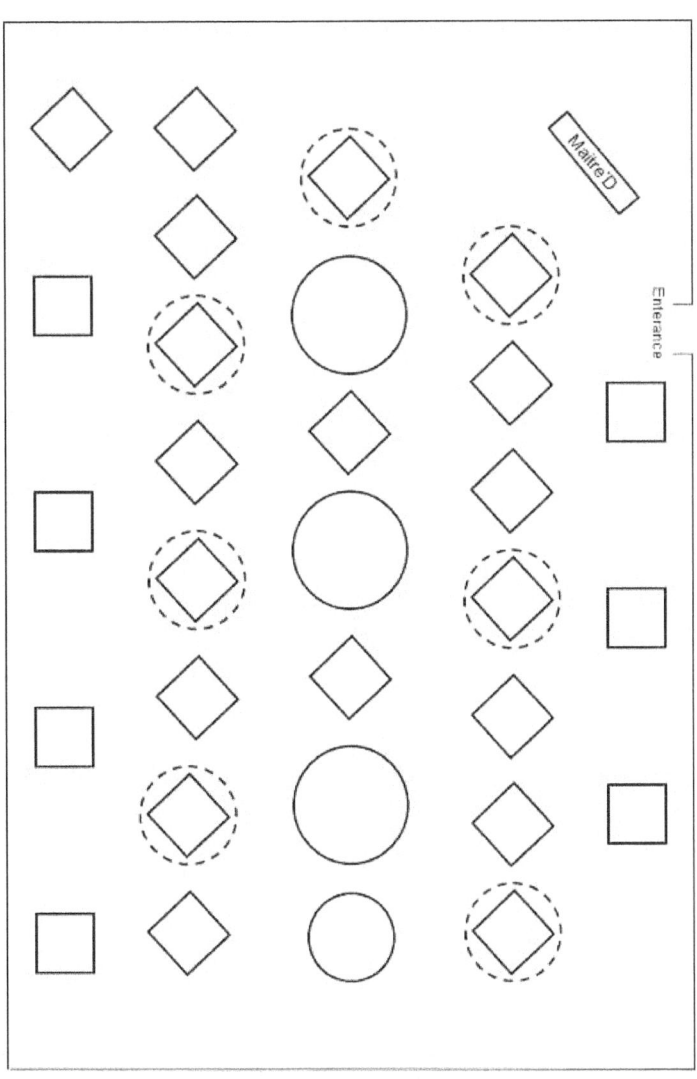

Station Breakdown

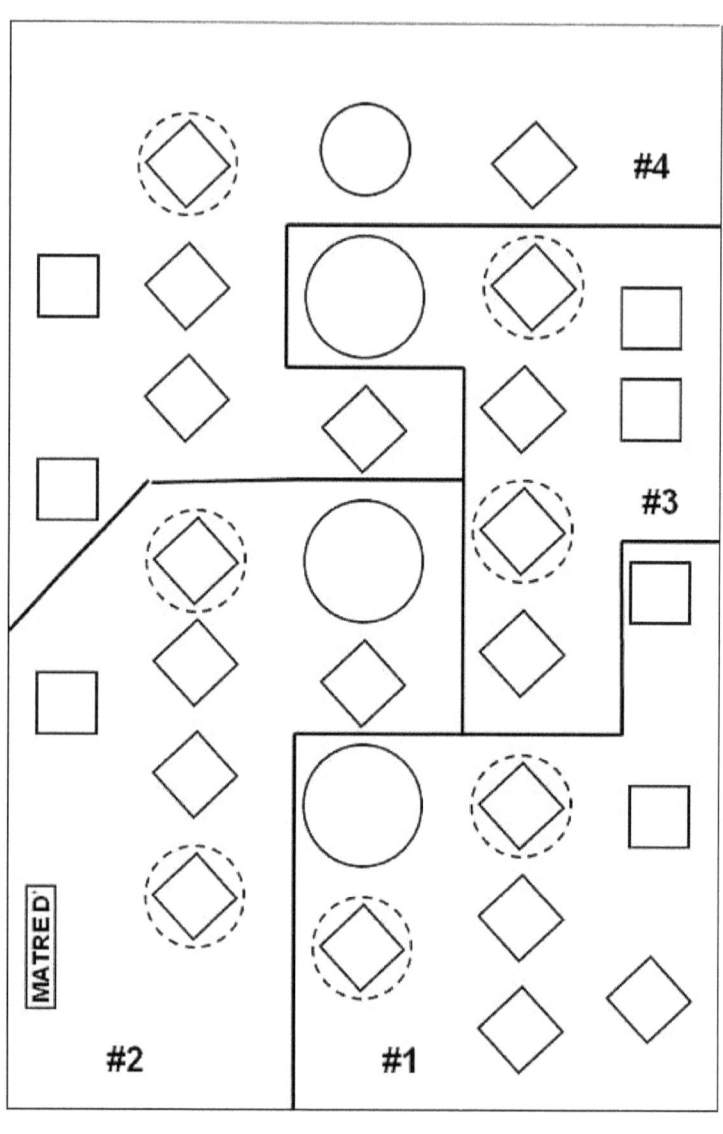

7 of 2 = 14
12 of 4 = 48
7 of 6 = 42
4 of 8 = 32

2 of 2 = 4
3 of 4 = 12
2 of 6 = 12
1 of 8 = 16

B. Main Dining Room and Reservations

When a person takes the time and effort to make a lunch or dinner reservation, the caller should expect confirmed seating unless he/she is told that no availability exists. Seating for persons who just walk in creates a guessing game for the Maitre d'. Maybe there is a table available or that a table is ready to be reoccupied.

The best advice to give persons willing to wait is to recommend that they might enjoy a cocktail in the bar until their table is ready. Many guests welcome the idea of waiting while seated at the bar. It is also good for business. Others will refuse and be willing to wait otherwise. They should be seated when the first table becomes available especially if they have to wait while standing.

When the time for the party in the bar is ready to be seated, many hosts will carry their own drinks to the table, however many will not if escorted by ladies. The lounge server or bartender should offer to carry their drinks to the table. This is the earmark of quality service.

When the party is seated the lounge server or bartender should ask if an additional round of drinks is desired. This gives the station server extra time to approach if the station server is busy.

The menu should be presented open to each person from the right with the right hand. Our main concern is to create a reputation for quality; the lifeblood of any establishment.

A knowledgeable staff promotes consistency of good food and service to new customers and existing club members. People are willing to pay prices on the menu but also expect a high level of service and delicious food.

There will be times when we drop the ball, not intentionally, but by unfortunate circumstances such as when staff does not show for duty. When a station is struggling to keep up, a trained server should, in a pleasant way, inform the guest that there will be a short delay in service.

As long as the guest is informed and aware of the situation guests are more willing to tolerate some delay and slow service but only to a certain point; before they find themselves rebelling. A server's negative facial expression, tone of voice, and surly personality will definitely entice the host to complain especially when this happens on a single server station.

The System

There is a proven system with which any difficult situation previously mentioned can be corrected and indeed almost avoided if adopted for the benefit of an entire dining room. This system I highly recommended and it should be added to the actual operational budget.

The additional expense is worth every penny for the establishment's food and service reputation. The system calls for scheduling an extra server who is without a station responsibility.

This is called a "mister floater" whose job it is to assist any server in need - from taking an order, assisting in service, helping to clear a table for a second seating, and carrying the second tray from the kitchen for service to a larger table. This "mister floater" also oversees the entire room operation looking for any sign of anyone needing assistance in any way.

"Mr. Floater" can be a dining room service staff member who is scheduled in rotation from the dining room or an experienced steady banquet server wishing extra time. By paying only one dollar over the minimum wage per hour it is possible to secure good service on forecasted busy days or for other reasons when traffic is expected to be heavy. Unless a very successful place has heavy daily traffic, "Mr. Floater" can be the only answer to an unforeseen problem.

Damage is avoided not only for the party involved but also for the surrounding tables. In reality, these suggestions have proven very effective in improving service.

Gratuity Suggestions

No one absolute way is known as the perfect way to serve. Following the traditional way is the basic way to perfect service but must be in accordance with the establishment's type of adaptation to improve service.
A very important suggestion is to avoid a big problem by allowing an inclusive gratuity of 20% be added to the total bill. This type of practice is not recommended – not for personal reasons but for the following reasons:

1) The server taking the order will recommend the high priced items to increase the check's bottom line.

2) Guaranteeing such gratuity allows the server not to provide the best service possible since the server is not depending on guest satisfaction.
3) It has been practice to demand a certain amount of gratuity without the guest's approval.
4) It is good for the IRS in reporting gratuities and easy for the establishment's payroll department.

Many people are not aware of or overlook the addition unless the added percentage is clearly printed in bold letters and not hidden between the lines. The guest can refuse the added gratuity, by complaining to management, and then only paying the total less gratuities. If the service was satisfactory, the total plus gratuities can be paid accordingly. If not, the total is paid and the proper amount of gratuity is paid in cash because the mandatory gratuity was not equal to service received. This also provides good information to management and allows for further action.

C. Dining Room and Table Service

Today it is quite controversial whether to use standard or a personal service preference. It depends on whether traditionally the food is to be served from the left side of a person with the left hand or from the right with the right hand. Many people feel that the choice of service is up to the individual establishment.

The correct way is for the food to be served from the left with the left hand and clearing from the right with the right hand. All wine and drinks should be served from the right with the right hand always facing the guest.

There should be a standard in providing service in order to avoid confusion as to true service etiquette. The French serve from the right. It is their custom. Russians and Americans serve from the left.

It is strongly recommended managers in all disciplines observe the performance of:

1. Service methodology
2. Food quality
3. Appearance and performance of employees

D. **Professional Dining Room Service**

For truly professional service, the guest must receive the ultimate in service performed by a professional wait staff which features consistency in execution, tempo, cooperation, and most importantly, communication from top management down to the bus person. In professional service, every item from the cocktail glass, water, appetizer, main course, dessert, and coffee has a purpose, shape, character, and position of its own on each table. Each item must be properly handled, presented, and positioned – from placement to removal –avoiding the temptation to sacrifice service for the sake of speed. Speed is necessary but not to the degree that it is obvious by clearing half of the table and leaving the other half to be cleared ten minutes later or by serving from every direction, over the person's head, and across the table, or with pouring water and coffee sloppily.

Service

Do not rush taking the order, or to serve, or to clear. People enjoy a night out for a leisurely dinner. That said there will be times when the server is instructed about theatre times or other reasons. But never let the customer feel that dinner is being rushed. The majority of clubs and restaurants present the menu immediately after the party is seated and these menus should be presented closed. If the style of service dictates that no menu is presented when the party is seated, the host member will request the menu when the party is ready to order. At this time the menu should be presented open.

E. Serving and Clearing

1. After the order has been taken, it must immediately be taken to the kitchen.
2. At this time, place proper utensils dictated by the menu selections, i.e. cocktail or fish fork and knife, steak knife.
3. In placement, plates should not extend over the rim of the table and above all, carry only two dishes at a time.
4. Place all courses with regard to the plate's contents and place in a way so that the contents will face the diner correctly and uniformly. (Place the plate, then adjust to perfect positioning – a move of "care").
5. Handle all dishes with the thumb on the rim of the plate and hand.
6. If the plates are hot, use a folded napkin, not a loose one.
7. Always remember that the palm of the hand should face the person at all times.
8. Serve from the left with the left hand.
9. Serve ladies first in the order that the order was taken.
10. Garnish of lemon, tomato, or others should be positioned at two o'clock high.
11. Remove all empty cocktail glasses.
12. Present the pepper mill asking first if pepper is desired.
13. Check from time to time asking "is everything satisfactory."

Clearing

1. Clear from the right with the right hand but not crossing in front of the person.
2. Clear the entire table completely by removing not only used items but items as well which have no more use on the table such as salt and pepper shakers.
3. Do not clear more than two dishes at a time with the exception of adding butter dishes and utensils on top of dinner plates but do this behind the guest.
4. Never scrape food particles from plate to plate to allow for more room to carry more plates.

Dessert

1. Offer dessert from the menu or bring a service cart. Offer coffee or tea from a tea caddy from which various teas are available.
2. Offer after dinner drinks and cordials.

Placing Items

1. Tomato wedge on salad at two o'clock.
2. Soup cups on liner with handles at nine and two o'clock.
3. Pies with the point at six o'clock.
4. Smoked fish fillets placed long at nine and three o'clock.

Order of Service

1. Children or Ladies
2. Disabled
3. Gentlemen
4. Ladies
5. Host
6. Gentlemen
7. Host

Personal Tools of a Server

Our profession's tools are service oriented requiring the server to possess the following:

1. To have the knowledge to perform duties in a professional manner.
2. Have a positive attitude which will create a bond between self and guests.
3. To smile and always use eye to eye contact when talking to people – leave personal problems at home when dealing with everyone else.
4. Good language skills – addressing with "sir" or "ma'am" and answering with "yes sir" or "yes ma'am" (never say "there you go," "right on," "okay," "okie-dokie," "want to order?" etc.)
5. Consistency to perform all tasks in the same manner at all times.
6. Body language skills – moving and performing with freedom and grace.
7. Effort in service – attentive, visible, and available at all times.
8. Awareness so as not to stop short or stop dead or change direction instantly to avoid accidents,

especially with loaded trays of hot food and liquor which may cause serious injury. To server and patron.

9. Pleasing – taking the extra step and effort to please and immediately report to management all incidents that occurred (good or bad).

Service is an art. There is nothing more wonderful and satisfying for a person than to sit down to a fantastic meal accompanied by the perfect wine and be served in a flawless and professional manner. The meal is handled, served, and placed in position with flair and consistency. Here is the correct sequence in seating guests:

1. Pull the chair for the ladies and unfold the napkin from the left with the left hand and gently place it on the lady's lap.

2. The cocktail person now takes the order. If busy, the cocktail person should notify the host that he or she will be right with them. When approaching with greeting of the day and name of host, the server should ask if a cocktail is desired by looking at everyone (not the host) and then departing with a "thank you" only.

3. Do not present the menu unless requested. Do so only after the cocktails are served. Inquire of the host or hostess if he or she would desire to order now or would they prefer to wait a while. Do not present a wine list to host with the menu.

4. The opened menu should be presented clockwise from the host first presenting it to the ladies.

5. When the order is ready to be taken, start with the first lady moving counter-clockwise, and advancing to the host's left. Keep a respectable distance and repeat the order making sure the request is heard correctly.

6. Do not hold on to a chair, cross your legs, over bend, touch hair, or any other part of the body at any time during the course of service.

7. When taking the host's order, inquire if a wine is desired to complement the dinner, or if a glass of wine is desired to complement each item ordered. Immediately after the order is taken and the cocktail person is informed that wine is required, turn in the order to the kitchen for prompt preparation. To cover a small delay in service inform the guest who ordered time consuming items such as lobster or double lamb chops, that extra time is required. If the party is mixed, take orders in the following sequence:

    1. Children
    2. Disabled persons
    3. Ladies
    4. Men
    5. Host

If a cocktail server is not available, the captain or the person taking the order should act and perform in the same manner as specified previously. Be sure to explain the day's specials, if any. Ask: "How would you like your meat cooked, what type of dressing with your salad, what type of potatoes or vegetables" when there are choices. If name tags are a part of the uniform, it is not necessary to announce that your name is "Bruce" or "Carmen" and you will be their server tonight. The reservation card should be removed at this time, and say "enjoy your dinner."

Cocktail and Food Staff Do Not's and No-No's:

Chewing gum, food, or hard candy – may spill out while talking

Scratch any part of the body

Wipe face

Sneeze – excuse yourself and walk off the floor and return after washing hands

Hands in pockets or waistband

Crossing legs

Pull up apron or pantyhose

Blowing of nose

Bite nails

Pencil in mouth or on ear

Yawning

Bulging pockets with keys and change

Beepers

Folding arms

Holding to a chair

Touch hair for any reason

F. Incident Report

An incident report should be standard operating procedure in documenting complaints, compliments, and suggestions by the member of customer to insure that an incident is acknowledged with the implied belief that action will be taken

INCIDENT REPORT FORM

Date: _____

Time_____

Location_____

Reason for report_____

Reported by_____

Position_____

Description_____

_____

_____

_____

_____

_____

_____

_____

Signed_____

Print Name_____

CHAPTER 5

TAKING THE ORDER

A. Cocktail and Wine Service

Be sure to approach and acknowledge the presence of guests with a smile. Not a contrived smile. Greet the host by name and by time of day, standing to the right of host making eye contact with all guests while taking the order in a counter-clockwise direction. By looking at the next person and acknowledging the person as "ma'am", "madam", or "sir", it is not necessary to go around taking each order. But make sure with each order to mark from one to ? and by X mark (x1, x2, etc.) for persons to be served first to avoid having to ask who receives what. Serve the ladies first from a cocktail tray lined with a napkin, positioning the cocktail to the right of the guest on a cocktail napkin with the logo or design facing the guest. At all times it is a must to carry a tray to clear empty glasses. Also inquire if another drink is required and never, never remove or carry empty glasses with bare hands. This is the reason for carrying a tray. When serving, clearing, or resetting a table; all glassware is to be handled from the middle of the cocktail glass with the two forefingers and from the middle of the glass for other glasses. Never pick up a glass of any kind with your fingers touching the top of the glass.

In the event wine is ordered and no matter how low priced it might be, the server should always compliment the host for his fine choice. He/she might not know wines or not be willing to order expensive wines. Your compliment in front of his guests will be greatly appreciated by his ego and for the gratuity later. The

order should always be taken with only a "thank you".
Do not say, "I will be back with your drinks in a moment
or I will be right back." Just simply say, "thank you."
Be attentive, visible, and available by scouting the
dining room or your section for a raised hand or to
notice that someone is looking around in need of
something or if the host is serving wine to his/her
guests. Attend to it immediately or inform the
sommelier, if one is on duty, and work together. If the
cocktail server is responsible for both cocktails and
wines, many times he/she will depend on the service
staff for help in pouring wine and for informing the
cocktail server of the need for additional drinks. When
wine is ordered and served execution becomes art

When the type of wine is ordered, be sure that the
appropriate glasses are placed on a lined tray and
never brought to the table between fingers. If both
white and red wines are ordered, usually the white wine
will be served first. The wine glasses should be placed
to the right with the white wine first in line below the red
wine glass. First a bucket should be placed to the right
of the host ¾ full of ice cubes and water which allows
for easy insertion of the bottle. To speed cooling, if the
wine is not already cold, add rock or plain salt to the ice
and water.

When presenting the wine it should be held in the palm
of the left hand on a folded napkin turned on a forty-five
degree angle with the side of the label facing the host
so they can inspect and verify the wine selection. The
bottle then should be inserted into the iced bucket and
the tip of the foil cut just above the rim and just below
the top of the bottle, placing the foil in your pocket and
not in the bucket. The sound of a bottle of wine being
opened somehow adds atmosphere to the room in
which case the louder the pop the better.   The

host/hostess should be served first with approximately two ounces of wine being poured to taste for approval. Once approved, then serve the rest of the guests starting with ladies first and moving counter-clockwise around the table.

Constantly refilling a half glass will keep the wine cold and crisp to drink. Return the bottle to the bucket stand with the towel draped across the top. If the bottle is empty <u>do not insert</u> the neck into the bucket. Inquire about a refill. If none is desired, remove the stand and bucket. Red wines should be presented and served in the same fashion as white wines. All red wines should be handled gently and with care so as to not disturb any sediment through rough handling. This is especially true of aged red wines in that they require extreme care to avoid disturbing the sediment at the bottom of the bottle. Rough handling of old wines will result in the wine becoming cloudy. The proper method for red wine is for the bottle to be carefully placed in a wine basket, lined with a napkin in such a way that the corner of the napkin is placed directly underneath the tip of the bottle's neck to catch any dripping. The bottle should then be presented with the label facing the host/hostess for approval. The wine is to be placed on the table to the right side of the host/hostess whether in a basket or standing and is not to be removed during opening. The top of the foil is then cut just below the bottle's head using the corkscrew's knife. Put the foil in your pocket and insert the corkscrew all the way into the cork. Pull, unscrew and present cork, wet side up, to the right of the host/hostess to sniff and approve. Clear head of bottle with napkin and pour two ounces of wine for the host/hostess to taste and approve. Then pour half a glass to the guests starting with the ladies first moving counter-clockwise. <u>Do not</u> allow the neck of the bottle to touch the glass while pouring. Twist the bottle slightly to avoid dripping and wipe neck of bottle with napkin before pouring to next guest. When the bottle is empty, inform host and ask if another bottle is desired. If not, remove basket or bottle. Many aged red wines are best decanted into special wine decanters. This must be done very slowly to avoid disturbing the wine's sediment which will cloud the wine if disturbed.

B. The Sommelier

Wine service is just as complex as the wines themselves. From high priced vintage to plain table wine, service should be handled with professionalism.

Presenting, decanting, serving, pouring or refilling all deserve flair and grace. Not in the same fashion as pouring water.

The majority of private clubs, upscale restaurants and hotels have the luxury of employing professional sommeliers and wine stewards to perform wine service and to maintain wine cellars containing more than a 2000 bottle inventory.

Many sommeliers are talented enough so that they can actually identify types and names of wines without reading the bottle label. They are capable of offering or suggesting the proper wine with all types of food.

A sommelier looks distinguished with a silver chain and cup around the neck in order to taste the wine first for its quality before offering a taste to the host.

When new wines are to be purchased, the General Manager or sommelier should assemble a group of selected staff members to sample the new wines for color, aroma, taste, quality, and price prior to making purchase. See Appendix

C. The Tray and Tray Jack

The Tray

Service trays and tray jacks are the server's most usable tool.

Assortments in tray sizes are designed for an assortment of duties and there is a reason for their sizes and shapes.

No trays of any kind must enter a dining room without being lined with a napkin and with a folded table cloth wrapped around the tray jack.

Absolutely no tray is to be placed or rested on a tray stand in the middle of a dining room next to a table to be served with the only exception being for clearing after the party has departed.

No tray is ever to be carried like a toy empty, or in a vertical position, resting on a hip, or overhead with two hands or ever tucked under one's arm. Never rush or run with it.

Do not overload a tray (maximum eight covered dishes) and place loads from center to each edge of tray for balance.

Rest a tray on tray jack only in a parallel position.

Do not lift or rest a loaded tray with two hands from the erect or bent position. Make sure that the tray is centered over the jack's wooden bars.

Do not stack up coffee cups and saucers on top of one another.

When going through doors hold the tray in the opposite direction (you may back through the door holding the tray with both hands) and be on alert for unexpected interference while walking on the right side of the aisle.

The Tray Jack (Stand)

The tray jack is designed to be folded and carried with ease.

The only time tray jacks are allowed in the dining room is to clear a used table, or for resting trays for dirty dishes from the pantry to the dishwashing area.

All tray jacks are to be skirted when being taken into the dining room to clear a table.

Lined tray jacks belong in all service areas only to rest trays and to serve food from there to the table, and never next to the table. Lined tray jacks are allowed in the room but are to be placed only in strategic areas and away from the dining tables.

Correct Water Service

Water is the very first item that diners receive without having to ask and it starts the overall structure of service in detail even before diners order. Consistency and inconsistency will be a clear indication to a member or restaurant diner of the type of service that they are inclined to receive for the rest of their meal. After the greeting, water is the first contact between the server and diner or member. Invariably a service-minded diner will observe and form an impression about the quality of the service based upon how professionally the water is first poured. There are no assorted ways for serving water. There is only one way – the proper and professional way.

1. Pour from the right of each person.
2. Use a napkin and pour low into the glass to avoid splashing.
3. Do not fill the glass to the very top.
4. Constantly refill glasses throughout the meal.
5. Pour from the front of the pitcher and guard.
6. If using a bucket and tongs, the bucket must rest on a lined plate.
7. If available, use water pitchers without the ice guard on the nozzle. To pour without ice in the glass is acceptable if the glass is continuously refilled with ice cold water. NOTE: For extra special service, remove the old water glasses after dinner and return with fresh glasses with ice and filled with fresh water. This is time consuming when the service is busy but what a wonderful way to show that the extra step is meant to please, especially during slow times.

Incorrect

1. Lifting the glass off the table and pouring water and ice from the side of the pitcher.
2. Scooping ice from ice bucket into glasses and then pouring the water.
3. Refilling by lifting glass off the table.
4. Bringing already full, ice water glasses to the table initially is acceptable for banquets or large parties only.

Exceptions

1. There are establishments with a "no water unless asked for" policy.
2. Having bad tasting local water or requesting bottled water for personal reasons. In this case, add ice to the glass with bucket and tongs, then place the opened water bottle to the right of the glass.
3. Having a "no water unless asked for" policy because of a water shortage or to entice the diner to select other saleable choices, however "enticing" this is a bad policy unless there is a shortage of water in the area.
4. Reaching across the table to pour if it is not possible to get behind the diner such as corner booths.

E. Bread and Butter

Bread is regarded around the world as a necessary source of food for all meals or it can be a meal in itself. In America (the nation of plenty) bread is treated as a secondary item and is available in many different forms. Bread may be substituted for rice, potatoes, corn and pastas because of diet restrictions or simply by customer choice. In American dining rooms bread is expected to be served without asking - whether placed on the table or offered and presented with the meal.

Bread

1. Bread is to be served from a bread basket lined with a napkin (split fold) resting on a lined plate or a small oval platter.
2. Serve <u>hot</u> and on time.
3. Serve from the left with the right hand (no knuckles) and placed on the butter plate (not on dinner plate).
4. Serve with tongs or service spoon and fork.
5. Place right side up.
6. Preferably passed with the salad or main course and passed as often as possible.
7. Do not pre-set bread on the table. If too busy to pass, place basket on table with all breads right side up.

Butter

1. Butter is to be served as soon as guests are seated and placed next to two pre-set crackers on the butter plate.
2. Do not pre-set butter on plates or pre-set dish with butter.

3. Serve hard and cold butter from a glass or metallic bowl with a fork resting on a napkin lined plate.
4. Follow a pattern of uniformity when placing on plate.
5. Serve two butter patties per person.
6. Pass additional butter patties as required or requested.
7. Save unused butter and return to kitchen when closing.

F. The Napkin

There are multiple ways to fold a napkin as there is no standard to follow. Usually the dining room Maître d will adopt a fold to show the establishment's logo.

Other than the dining room and for any other occasion the napkin fold style or design would be up to the service manager's or supervisor's direction. Bear in mind that the napkin is handled and folded by bare hands into a specific design.

Please note specially folded long bent in half napkins inserted into a goblet from which guests are going to drink will leave marks and plenty of lint. It might be good looking but it is also unorthodox and unacceptable for a proper table setting.

Unfortunately, the napkin is the most disrespected item in the linen inventory and is also the most misused other than for its intended use.

A fan folded napkin is most attractive when placed above the logo on the service plate or across the plate. The fan fold looks good and is easy to handle.

Sadly, a clean napkin is often used as a rag to clean shoes, hands, stains, floor, silverware, wiping tables, and trays to name just a few misuses. Like all linen, a napkin is very expensive to launder. Clean rags should be made available in large quantities to use in the place of a clean napkin. Use of these clean rags demand close supervision and enforcement by management.

Spending valuable time for a very fancy design fold for only the looks of it requires one to consider the time invested and the proper setting in which it will be used. Using a double folded napkin is the correct item way to "crumb" a table instead of using fancy silver scrapers, knives, plastics or other types of scrapers.

G. Champagne

A bottle of champagne contains six atmospheres of pressure which is about the pressure of an inflated truck tire. The pressure makes opening a bottle of champagne a dangerous task if it is opened incorrectly.

Here are the steps to correctly open a bottle:

1) Break and remove the foil from the top of the bottle but leave the wire cage intact around the cork. You may choose to wrap the bottle with a clean napkin or a special towel just in case of spillage.
2) Place your thumb or your hand on top of the cork and leave it there until the cork has been removed.
3) With your other hand remove the wire cage by untwisting the wire about six turns. Be sure to continue keeping your thumb or hand firmly on the cork.
4) Tilt the bottle on a $45°$ angle, twist the cork in one direction and the bottle in the other direction, and ease the cork out of the bottle. Done properly the cork should never "pop" but rather make as Frenchmen say, "The contented sigh of a woman in ecstasy."
5) Hold the base of the bottle with one's thumb in the punt (a bottle's bottom indentation) and pour the champagne into the glass within one inch from the top of the glass.
6) Place any remaining un-poured champagne into the wine bucket which has been filled with ice and water.
7) Re-top the glasses only when one sip remains in a glass.

8) Never turn an empty bottle upside down in the bucket.
9) Ask if another bottle is desired. If not, remove the bottle and bucket.

H. Coffee Service

Around the world and especially in America, coffee is never to be underestimated as just a cup of coffee. To many, it is the hallmark of fine dining whether it is the morning, night, or in a club or restaurant. People will treat their coffee according to their personal preference by adding the desired amount of items to make for themselves that perfect cup of coffee to enjoy. Out of the clear blue sky here comes the server or bus person adding more coffee without first asking, thus ruining the person's coffee experience. It is just a cup of coffee but if we ask five different servers to serve a cup individually maybe only one would serve it properly. Coffee for dining rooms should not be brewed until the room is ready to receive guests. Not two hours before. It takes only half an hour before acidity starts to form, making the coffee bitter.

Serving the Coffee:

1. Do not preset cups at dinner.
2. Do not place the teaspoon in the saucer.
3. Preferably use long neck coffee pitchers three-fourths full.
4. Guard the diner with folded napkin when pouring.
5. Do not fill the cup to the top, only fill three-fourths full.
6. Pour no higher than one inch from the cup.
7. Do not lift cup off the table.
8. Always ask before refilling a cup.
9. Do not fill creamers to the top.
10. Do not preset sugars and cream until coffee is requested.

11.   Place the cup and saucer four inches from the rim of the table with the handle at four o'clock.

I. Sorbet

Another former course of gourmet service was the presentation of a sorbet. This service still exists in five star establishments or when requested by the host.

Based on the chef's creation, sorbets may be a variety of fruits and herbs and are used to clear the diner's palate. They may be served after the appetizer or before the main course. Both ways are accepted practice.

A small scoop of sorbet is served in a glass dish or in a silver champagne saucer type of dish and then placed on a silver or china base. The size being that of butter dish which is lined with a doily and served with a tea spoon on the plate pointing at 11 o'clock.

This is a very unique item.

J. Finger Bowl

The finger bowl is the last item to be served. In gourmet service, the finger bowl is set on an eight inch silver plate lined with a doily, filled with a quarter inch of warm water and with a slice of lemon which is then presented for the guest to dip their fingers. A quarter folded clean napkin is placed to the left of the bowl. Finger bowls can also be served using all china or all glass settings.

Some fine establishments continue to do finger bowl service while others use the finger bowl only if the dinner had Maine lobster or food in which the guests had to use their fingers. Other establishments now use a wet warm napkin on a plate along with a clean napkin next to it while others do nothing at all.

Finger bowls too are very unique items.

CHAPTER 6

TYPES OF SERVICE

A. French Service

French service requires a truly professional staff: From the supervisory staff to the bus person.

From the time the order is taken, it should immediately be delivered to the kitchen for prompt preparation. The order may contain items from the menu which may be pre-plated in the kitchen or plated at table side or both. If both, timely service is essential to coincide with the table service preparation and the plated items from the kitchen along with hot plates for the table side items.

Orders taken for table side preparation performed by a chef, chef's assistant, or by the station trained Captain was once very popular. Food was presented on platters placed on a rolling guerdon or cart covered with a table cloth containing a lit sterno heater, carving board, carving and slicing utensils, clean napkins, peppermill, salt and necessary spices.

After the presentation, the chef or Captain would prepare items in flat crepes suzettes type pans until the food was cooked and portioned and plated; then sliced, carved, or deboned and placed on hot plates which came with the rest of the order from the kitchen.

B. Russian Service

Russian service is almost the same as French service with the exception being its simplicity as it is fully prepared and precut. Food is placed on silver platters for the servers to pass to each guest to choose the portion of choice, giving the guest that special attention.

The platter of food is placed on the table for self service whether portioned or served is by choice. To serve properly the server should hold the platter with the left hand and serve with the right hand. The only exception is that the platter is always presented to the host and then to the guests for approval and show.

Hot plates are placed first from the right with the right hand and served from the left. In the event that different items are chosen, each one should be served from a small platter.

C. American Service

American service is a combination of style preparation and service derived mostly from the French service but contains elements that the food is prepared and plated individually in the kitchen rather than plated at table side. It is most important for the server to load the tray by the way the dinner is located. The food is to be served by placing the dishes in line with orders as they were taken. This will avoid shuffling to find the right plate. The experienced server should offer the same courtesy and manner to the inexperienced diner who does not possess the knowledge of proper service.

The basic table service is French oriented for every establishment with table service but with many different adaptations to the true French service concept.
Authentic adaptations of true French service (gourmet service) have sharply declined from the past and now can only be found in upscale establishments.

The fast food industry took over the busy American schedule; lower cost in food, labor, and high turn in value led persons being given a tray with food and a cup to pour their own beverages. They are allowed to choose their own table, clear their own table, and no gratuities are involved.

CHAPTER 7

PREPARATION AND BASIC SERVICES

A. Gourmet Cooking

Successful gourmet cooking is the ultimate achievement in taste, quality, preparation, and presentation when it is followed by flawless, perfectly timed service that is performed professionally by service members.

The Chef

Every kitchen, small or large, has a chef. A gourmet chef is a professional individual who possesses a skill that he or she has learned and developed in a specific way by combining sauces, exotic and domestic herbs and spices and by selecting the choicest parts of meat, seafood, fowl, game, along with an array of foodstuffs needed to create a culinary masterpiece.

WHITE STOCK (Made from veal, fish, and chicken bones)

    1. Béchamel – made with milk or cream, cheese
    2. Volute – made with wine, curry, mushrooms

BROWN STOCK (Made from bones and drippings of roasts)

    1. Espanola – made with brown stock, red wines (Bordelaise)

TOMATO STOCK (Tomato products with all stocks)

    1. Hollandaise – made with eggs, lemon, butter, spices

2. Béarnaise – made with a reduction of vinegar, wine, tarragon, shallots and finished with egg yolks and butter

Depending on the chef's talent and creativity multiple varieties of sauces can be made from these basic sauces.

The Gourmand

The word gourmand (French) defines a person who knows, appreciates, and affords specially prepared foods and the fine wines chosen to accompany a creation. The true gourmand is generally flexible in terms of choice yet the most critical in terms of taste. He or she refuses to compromise quality, preparation, price, and professional service.

The originator of gourmet cooking was a Frenchman named Brillat Savarin who fled to America during the French Revolution. When he went back to France he formed a society and developed the classical terms of gastronomy, giving it the name "The Physiology of Taste."

Types of Service

There are three types of standard methods of service:

FRENCH   (tableside service)

Each course is brought on individual silver platters and served to each guest by a server from platter to hot plate. Carved or cooked tableside from a guerdon cart to plate and served by a server.

RUSSIAN   (family service)

Assorted courses in platters placed on tables to be passed from person to person so each can help themselves.

AMERICAN

Pre-plated courses are served from a service area. This type of service also includes self-service from buffet with numerous items from which to choose.

CHAPTER 8

MEETINGS

A. Private Meetings

Private meetings are generally for a small number of persons however such meetings can be small in number, executive meetings, up to departmental meetings, or for an entire company.

Small meetings from four to fifteen persons can be accommodated in a 25' x 10' meeting room with only water being placed on a white cocktail napkin 12 inches from the rim of the table to the right of the chair as well as one or two iced water pitchers on a napkin lined plate in the middle of the table at equal distance to each other.

In the event that coffee and assorted pastries are to be included, a 6' to 8' table should be arranged for self service.

If a cold cut buffet or a plated luncheon is requested for more than ten persons, the meeting table must be preset before the meeting starts or set during a break.

For a cold cut luncheon, the server should have the table ready and be present for assistance and for any requests during the self service.

For any type of meeting, tray jacks are not to be in the room at any time. All service should be done from the next room if available or from outside the meeting room. This includes the clearing of dishes.

The server should not be in and out of the room during the meeting; and only called upon by the host to enter.

Meetings of any kind are very profitable with low labor and food cost. Additionally, extra revenue is generated from the room rental.

Buffets are very popular – from small to very large parties. They offer an extensive array of foods: from oriental, ethnic, and the all American buffet which frequently will feature unique specialties which might be unfamiliar to people from other parts of the country. An example would be grits with cheese; an item unknown to New Yorkers. Local buffets of any kind on weekends are favorites with American families; low key and inexpensive where a family can indulge and socialize at a moderate cost.

Elaborate buffets are top notch affairs featuring the best in quality food products. This type of buffet requires a great deal of preparation with cooks wearing tall toques standing behind the line accompanied by white gloved server; expensive skirting, and a rise every six feet with ice carvings and array of fine flowers.

Silver bowls of caviar, smoked sturgeon, lump crabmeat, lobster tails and sliced tenderloin are part of the culinary display. Desserts complete the buffet and include desserts cooked to order at various stations depending on the number of guests.

To offer this type of buffet requires the very best in silver equipment which has been designed for use in ornate ballrooms. This type of elaborate buffet demands a well trained service staff capable of providing top notch service.

To be clear, this book is not written to follow the exclusive type of buffets but rather it is written for the benefit of the all American weekend or Sunday buffet which is offered by most establishments. Small private groups or family get-togethers using private dining rooms find that buffets offer an array of food choices. For small or large groups, the banquet coordinators first and most important task is to present to the host/hostess various choices of buffet table designs from which to choose specifying a single or double line buffet and locations of bars, soups and desserts.

It is highly recommended as a procedural issue for very large buffets and banquets that the chef or sous-chef be present during the planning process to give his professional advice and to make suggestions that insure that the host enjoys a successful event.

It is important to remove all used items, especially when a guest has finished with a course and returns with more food. Each assigned station requires one server per 25 to 30 guests.

In the event no flowers have been ordered for the buffet table, a very effective method for the establishment is to place stems of fresh ferns in between the items on the buffet table.

A $10.00 investment in ferns will be noticeable to the host and guests. The ferns can be refrigerated after the function and be reused again for another event since refrigerated ferns can last as long as two weeks.

When an entire table has emptied, the assigned server should bring a lined tray jack and tray to use in clearing the table. Using the proper method for handling, the server removes and places glasses, plates, and silverware separately on the tray. Never use bus bins to clear a table at any time; not only for sake of appearance but most importantly, the bin does not have the capacity to separate items as does a tray thus forcing the staff to overload items on top of one another which in turn causes breakage and possible injury to the dishwasher.

When a table has been cleared, the table cloth should not be removed at this time until all guests have departed.

Here are some extremely important budgeting issues and recommendations for banquets and all the other service areas. Every department operates under a budget for monetary control with perhaps an extra allowance given to food and beverage areas in order to achieve the most maximum success.
Many establishments operate without a budget. They do so by looking at weather forecasts, weekend and holiday traffic, and other name dates to schedule weekly or daily staffing requirements. Thus saving a few dollars when scheduling servers and keeping production to a minimum.

Using a method of number plus one less whether budgeted or not, is a practice that will not save money but instead tarnishes the quality of service and it also creates disorganization.

CHAPTER 9

BANQUETS

A.   The Team Leader

Banquets and Special Functions

In preparation, organization and supervision, for a function to be executed well, it is the responsibility of the team leader or supervisory staff member. The team leader is chosen and authorized by management to oversee other servers and is expected to follow rules and specifications. The team leader must be capable of supervising other servers with knowledge and respect. Team leader duties are to make sure that the necessary supplies are assembled in place and in accordance with the type of menu and set-up to include:

- Assign servers to specific stations and side duties.
- As directed by the F&B service director to instruct, oversee, and participate in room set-up, service, and clean-up.
- Introduce themselves and inquire into starting time, tempo of service, and any last minute instructions or wishes.

- See that lights are properly adjusted to suit the host.
- Close, keep open, or reopen bar after coffee service.
- Control room temperature along with aid from the F&B director.
- To ensure that when there is a speaker, no service staff leaves the room.
- Ensure that tables are not cleared or stripped at the end of a function until all guests have left.
- Instruct to save items from buffets and brunches by taking them to the kitchen. The chef can salvage many of them as well as butter, creams, breads, and other items.

TEAM LEADERS REPORT

DATE: _____   NAME OF TEAM LEADER: _____
ROOM: _____   NAME OF SUPERVISOR: _____

TYPE OF FUNCTION: ☐ Sit ☐ Party ☐ Reception ☐ Meeting ☐ Other _____

TIME: Cocktails ☐   Reception ☐   Meeting ☐   Meal ☐

NAMES OF STAFF:

_____   _____
_____   _____
_____   _____

1) What was the name? _____

2) Did you introduce yourself to the host? ☐ Yes ☐ No   If not, why? _____

3) What if any, special instructions were given by the host: _____
_____
_____

4) Was the room set-up on time?: ☐ Yes ☐ No   If not, why? _____

5) Side jobs ready?

☐ Salt and Peppers	☐ Butter	☐ Trays	☐ Bread Baskets
☐ Sugars	☐ Creams	☐ Garbage Can	☐ Iced Tea & Lemons
☐ Crackers	☐ Extra Silverware	☐ Carts	☐ Water Pitchers
☐ Water	☐ Ice	☐ Coffee Cups and Saucers	☐ Gloves
☐ Breads	☐ Liners	☐ Coffee Pitchers	☐ Coffee

6) Did the party start on time? ☐ Yes ☐ No   If not, why? _____

7) Was the kitchen notified? ☐ Appetizer ☐ Salad ☐ Main Course ☐ Not applicable

8) Did kitchen have food ready on time:? ☐ Yes ☐ No   If not, why? _____

9) Was service smooth? ☐ Yes ☐ No   If not, why? _____

10) Did the staff perform well? ☐ Yes ☐ No   If not, why and who? _____
_____
_____

11) Were there any complaints and/or compliments from the host? ☐ Yes ☐ No   Please describe comments.
_____
_____

12) Clean-up Checklist: ☐ Room ☐ Linen ☐ Bread Box ☐ Urn ☐ Floor

TEAM LEADER SUGGESTIONS, how can we improve?
_____
_____
_____

FOR MANAGEMENT USE ONLY" List of names of staff who were not on time:

_____	☐ Warning	☐ Suspension	☐ Separation
_____	☐ Warning	☐ Suspension	☐ Separation
_____	☐ Warning	☐ Suspension	☐ Separation

Manager's Comments: _____
_____

B. Suggestions for Banquet Service

1) Stand still during a prayer and the pledge of allegiance.
2) Avoid service of any kind during a speech by leaving the room.
3) Walk to the assigned station by using a straight pattern instead of zigzagging between tables or across an empty dance floor not in use. Serve head table from behind not from the front.
4) Walk erect to serve with steady hands to the sides and do not swing arms back and forth.
5) If white glove service is called for, make absolutely sure that the gloves are spotless. This is especially true of the right and left thumb.
6) No matter the type of uniform, it is to be buttoned.
7) Do not communicate loudly with other servers.
8) Tray jacks should be around the dinner area service stations and not between tables for the server's convenience.
9) Clear tables with as little noise as possible.
10) Communicate informing the liquor/wine/food server any requests made by guests.
11) When coughing or sneezing the server must leave the room and then come back a few minutes later.
12) Always carry a handkerchief – so very important.

One, Two, & Three Prong Service

One Prong Approach Service From Far End of Room

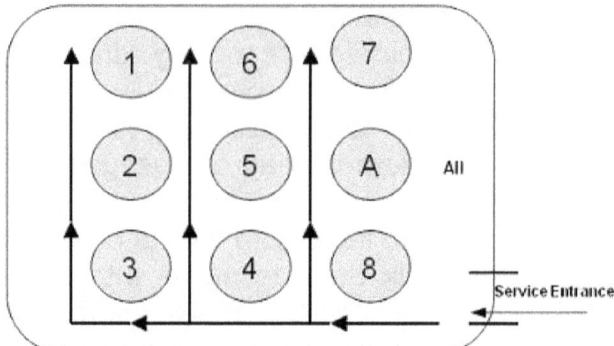

Two Prong Approach with Room Split in Two

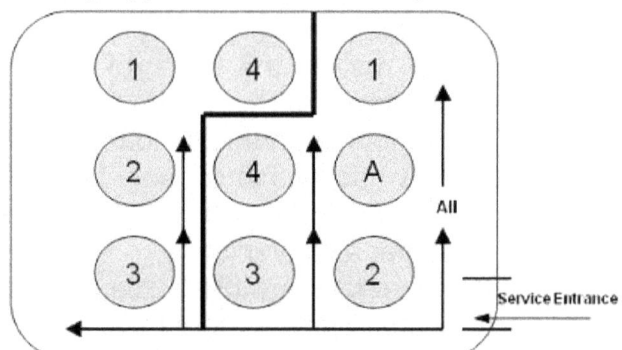

Three Prong Approach Service with Teams

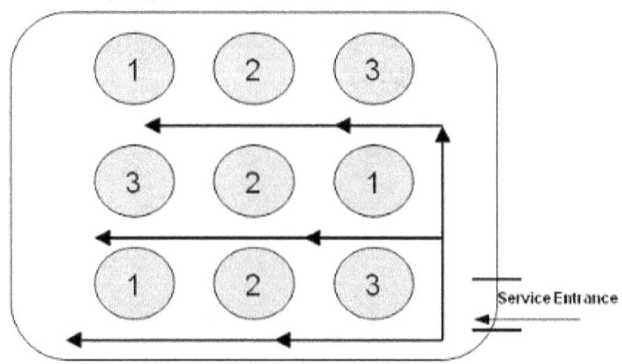

Service with a Dance Floor

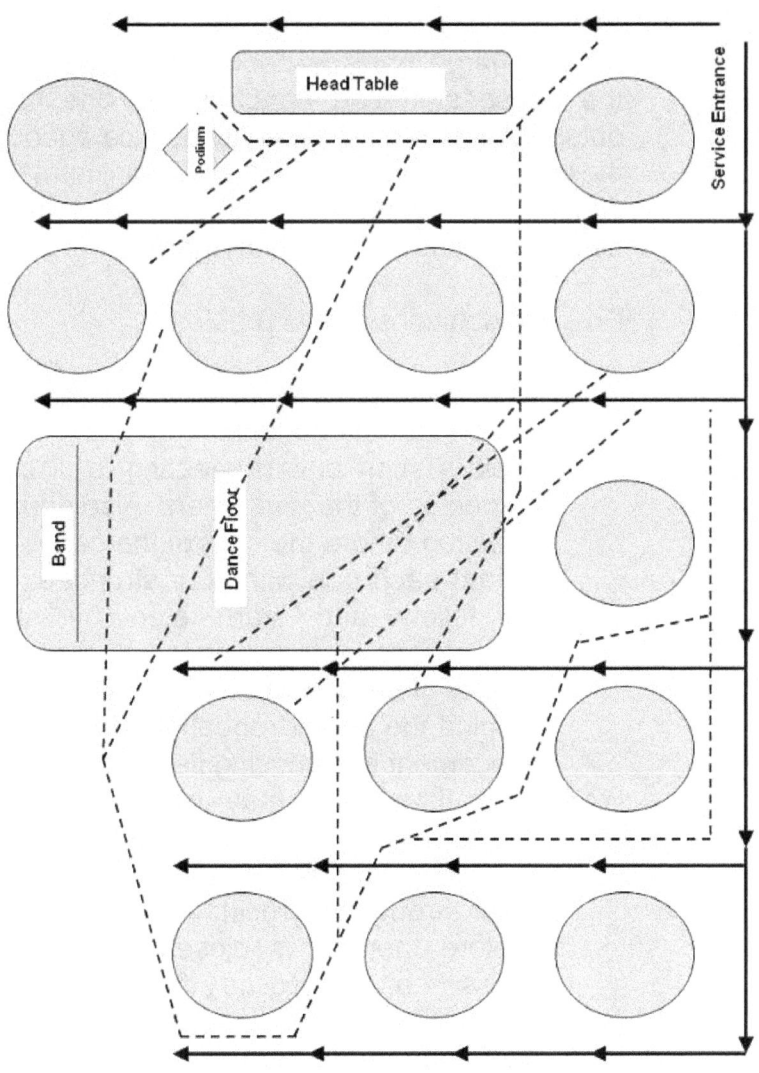

C. Part-time Hires

When a large party is booked for more persons than the house staff can handle, then one must employ outside help from a hospitality service agency. Some of these part-timers will have only minimum experience. Others may come from the fast food industry. This becomes a supervisor's nightmare.

Possible solutions to this problem:

1) Demand from the agency that people they hire report for duty on time.
2) Hold a short private meeting to discuss what is expected of the part timers. Also during the main meeting before the start of the party.
3) Team each hire with your strongest servers. So to follow and learn step by step how-to instructions: refilling water glasses, picking up empty glasses with a lined tray; follow in serving behind the server repeating the same method of placement or removing items.
4) Part time hires may relieve the server from performing side jobs, pass certain items, or they can start icing glasses in the service area half an hour through the cocktail hour.
5) Before the bar is closed, bring out the iced glasses on a lined tray for one table at a time. Place the glasses on the assigned table three inches from the top of the first knife. Pour water when all guests are seated.

D. Guest Greetings at Opening

Go the extra step to please whenever the opportunity arises. Guests will notice. It has been proven that the host/hostess will always be impressed when service staff is aligned (male, female, male, and female) on each side of the entrance to the banquet room in order to greet each guest with a smile as they enter the room. The greeter will say, "Good Afternoon" or "Good Evening." Never allow the host to look for management to give last minute instructions. Stay close within sight to comply immediately with the host's wishes. Suggest lighting (pink color lights on tables are internationally preferred by lady guests for it improves their complexion.) Inquire about the room's temperature or if soft taped music is available; or a live microphone might be required.

E. Preparation

A great deal of detail planning is required for proper execution of service. Be it a simple meeting, cocktail party, reception, banquet dinner, or gourmet meal requiring white glove service.

Banquet service should be performed with the same style and etiquette as dining room service. The only exception: a multitude of persons are served from a pre-set menu of three to seven courses.

Schedule

The service staff should be scheduled in advance and in accordance with the necessary requirements:

A. Two hours before the function, the required amount, type of tables, and number of chairs should be placed by a crew of housemen (if any), if not:

B. Two and one half hours before the function the servers are required to set up the tables and chairs.

C. Schedule the service staff three hours in advance if the staff is to have a meal before or after set-up.

D. Any server arriving late should be disciplined by assignment to pantry duty after dessert is served.

Preparation Follow Through

Example: Six servers are scheduled for a function for 72 guests - Jean (the team leader), Joe, Mary, Tom, Joseph, and Bill.

All must adhere and report for dinner on time. Supervisor in charge is Peter. The first duty is staff assignment and then pantry preparation by all staff.

Example of pantry and side job assignments:

Jean
Coffee and decaf
75 cups and saucers
Box of tea bags
6 coffee pots
2 pots for hot water

Tom
Salt and pepper shakers are full
18 lined bread baskets with tongs
3 iced tea containers and glasses
Quartered lemons
Tray lined with napkin with assorted silverware for replacement for any reason
Activate bread box with rolls or buns (help from supervisor)

Mary
20 butter plates (oval) with container of iced butter per table
18 sugar containers on a doily plate
1 4-tier Queen Mary with Trays
18 cream containers ¾ full,
(2 per table usually a dishwasher is assigned)

Joseph
80 water goblets lined box full of ice cubes
Remove glass and dirty dishes and resupply if
needed. Assignment is to service area duty.

Bill
3 - 8' long tables lined
1 bus box for used silver
12 oval service trays lined with
napkin
2 lined trash cans

Individual Table Responsibility

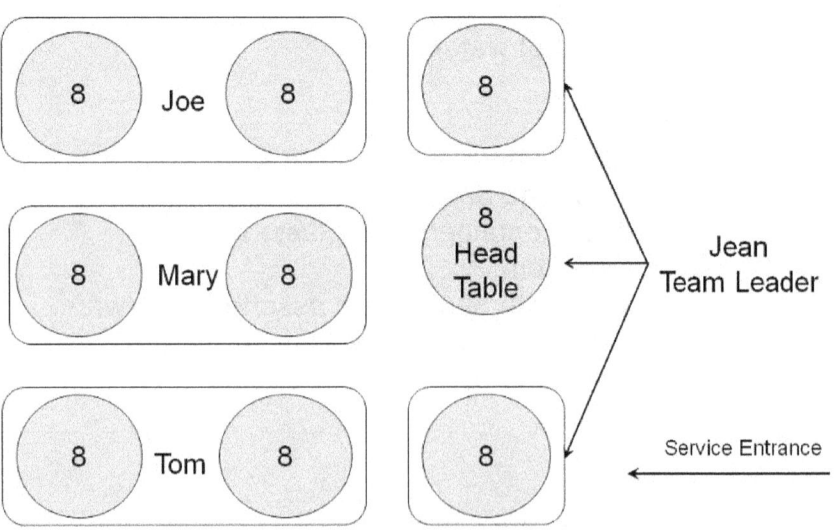

Post Request Sheets on Board

All plates, dishes, silverware, glasses, pitchers, pots, etc. to be ready in time for kitchen steward for prompt pick-up by service staff. Submit requisition for linen requirements. Submit floor diagram with specifications to housemen (if no housemen) post for early wait staff assignment. Post floor plan.

F. Set-up Method for Banquets

1. All staff members are to participate according to station assignment – day or night.
2. Display example of chosen menu set-up.
3. Pad a table first which is necessary.
4. Use proper sized tablecloth, checking all sides for evenness and seams facing the same direction on all tables.
5. Arrange chairs equal distance apart at all tables.
6. Clean chairs they should just be touching the tablecloth.
7. All silverware polished-a damp cloth with coffee is recommended – no acid or odor in coffee. Do not use <u>water.</u>
8. Base plate placed one inch from table's edge with crest right side up.
9. Napkin above logo or middle of base plate.
10. Never handle silverware with bare hands – use lined tray and napkin. Stand behind each chair and fine tune the silverware so that each piece is evenly spaced and parallel to each other in proper angles and wine glass below to the right of water glass.
11. All tables should have symmetry and be inspected by team leader or supervisor.
12. Butter plates placed at 11 o'clock of the base plate with the butter knife to the right of plate and directly above the highest fork according to standard or house design.

Place two saltines or crackers preferably lightly toasted on each plate.

Table Center

Place salt and pepper in one position on all tables with the salt to the right of pepper. In banquets butter should be preplaced on iced oval plates on a liner according to the number of guests at the table and then placed in the same uniform position on all tables.

SET-UP REQUEST SHEET

For Banquets and Private Parties

Steward: _____

Day of Function: _____

Type of Function: _____

Location: _____

Items#	Items
Base Plates	_____
Water Pitchers	_____
Dinner Plates	_____
Coffee Pitchers	_____
Salad Plates	_____
Chafing Sets	_____
Bread and Butter Plates	_____
Coffee Urns	_____
Coffee Cups and Saucers	_____
Tea Urns	_____
Creamers	_____
Tea Pots	_____
Sugar Bowls	_____
Water Glasses	_____
Butter Dishes Iced Tea	_____
Glasses	_____
White Wine Glasses	_____
Red Wine Glasses	_____
Beer Glasses	_____
Champagne Glasses	_____
Dinner Knives	_____
Steak Knives	_____
Butter Knives	_____
Dinner Forks	_____
Salad Forks	_____
Cocktail Forks	_____
Teaspoons	_____
Soup Spoons	_____
Iced Tea Spoons	_____
Fish Forks	_____
Fish Knives	_____

Additional Items

Buffet Dinner Table Set Up

Buffet Dinner Table

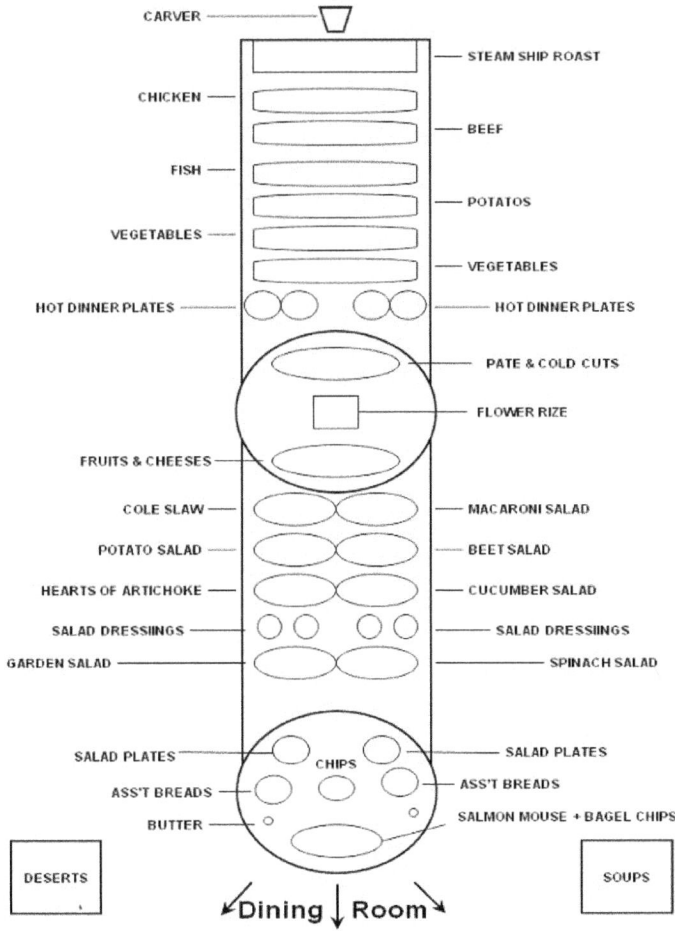

CARVER

STEAM SHIP ROAST

CHICKEN

BEEF

FISH

POTATOS

VEGETABLES

VEGETABLES

HOT DINNER PLATES — HOT DINNER PLATES

PATE & COLD CUTS

FLOWER RIZE

FRUITS & CHEESES

COLE SLAW — MACARONI SALAD

POTATO SALAD — BEET SALAD

HEARTS OF ARTICHOKE — CUCUMBER SALAD

SALAD DRESSIINGS — SALAD DRESSIINGS

GARDEN SALAD — SPINACH SALAD

SALAD PLATES — SALAD PLATES

CHIPS

ASS'T BREADS — ASS'T BREADS

BUTTER — SALMON MOUSE + BAGEL CHIPS

DESERTS

SOUPS

Dining Room

Buffet Setups

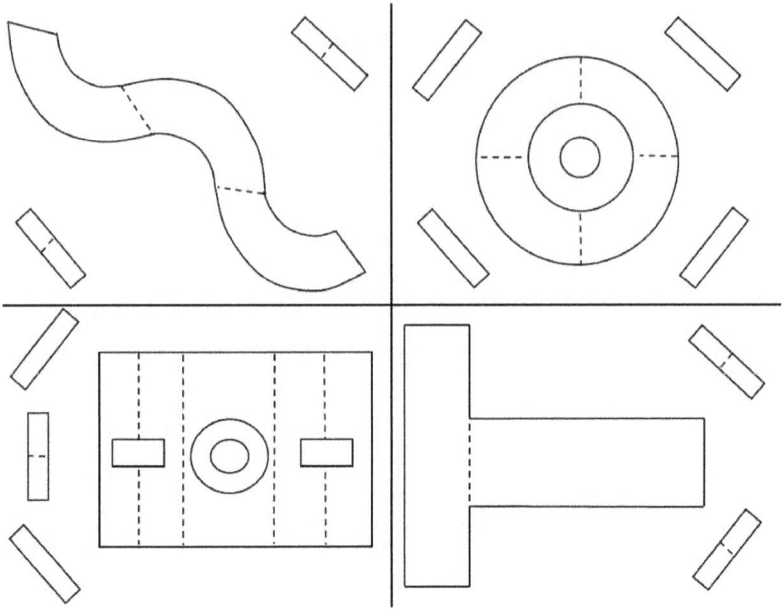

Buffet Setups

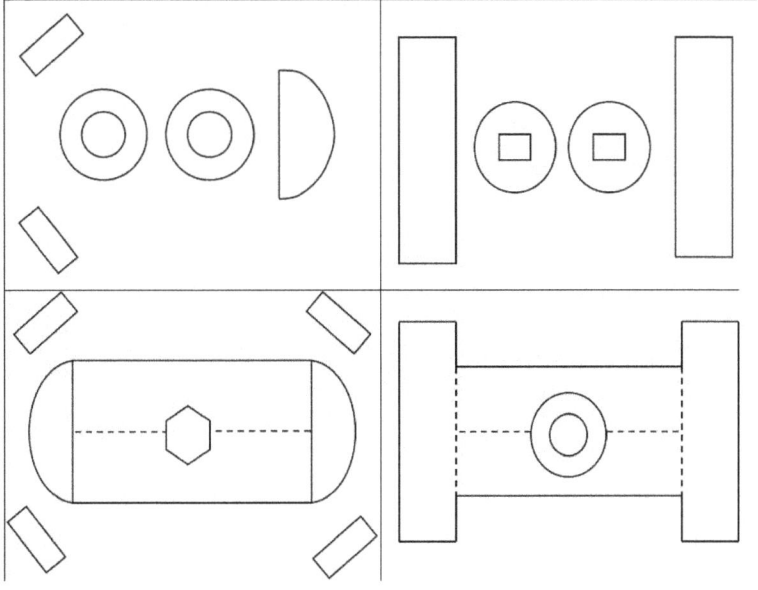

Buffet Setups

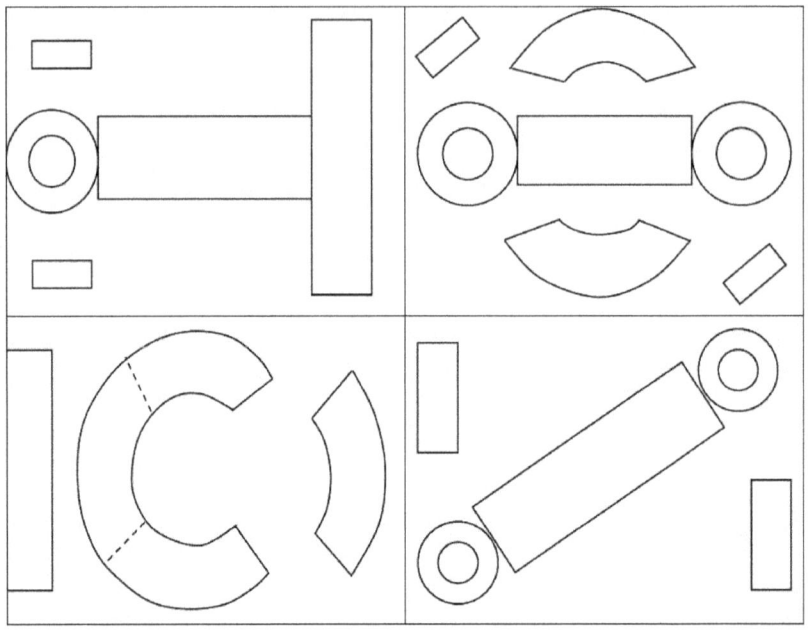

Buffet Set Ups

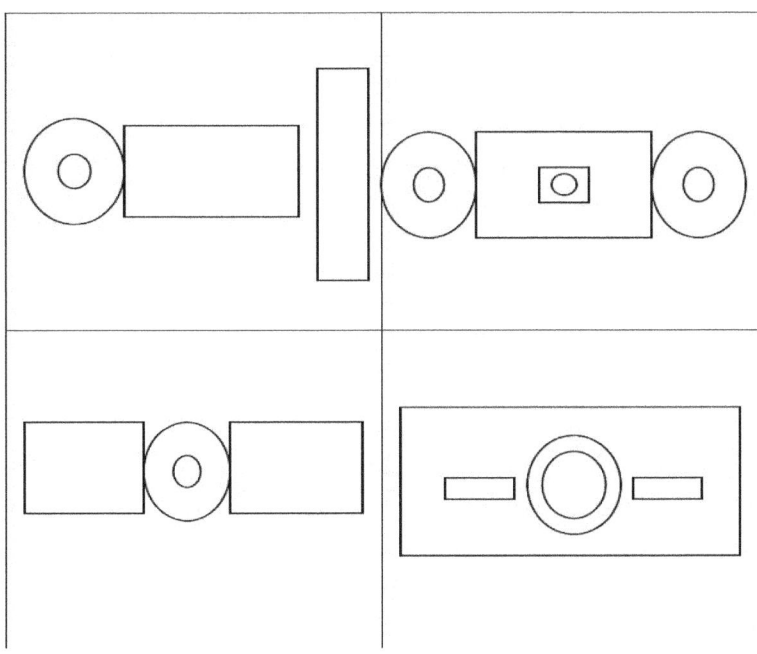

Buffet Brunch Set Up

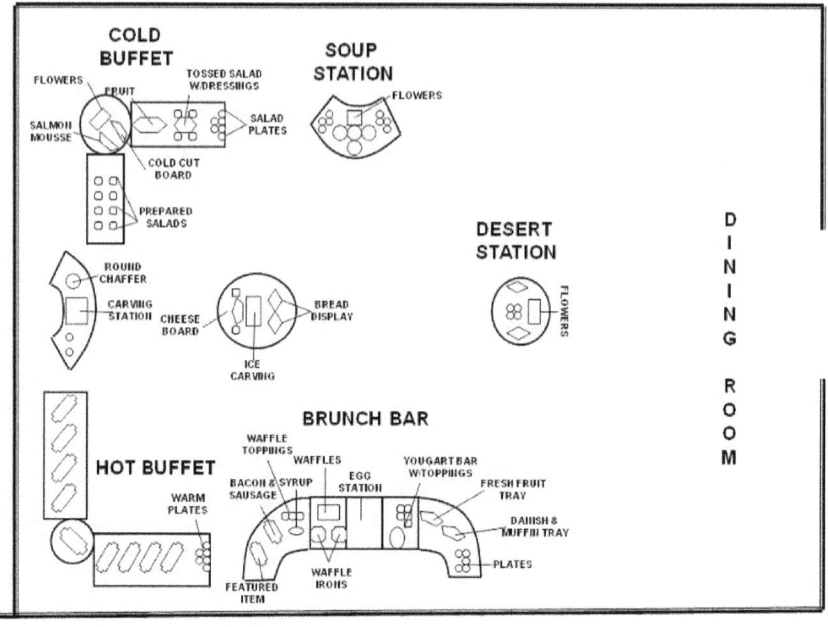

COLD BUFFET

FLOWERS
FRUIT
TOSSED SALAD W/DRESSINGS
SALMON MOUSSE
SALAD PLATES
COLD CUT BOARD
PREPARED SALADS

SOUP STATION
FLOWERS

DESERT STATION
FLOWERS

ROUND CHAFFER
CARVING STATION
CHEESE BOARD
BREAD DISPLAY
ICE CARVING

DINING ROOM

HOT BUFFET
WARM PLATES

BRUNCH BAR
WAFFLE TOPPINGS
WAFFLES
BACON & SAUSAGE
SYRUP
EGG STATION
YOUGART BAR W/TOPPINGS
FRESH FRUIT TRAY
DANISH & MUFFIN TRAY
PLATES
WAFFLE IRONS
FEATURED ITEM

Buffet Breakfast Set Up

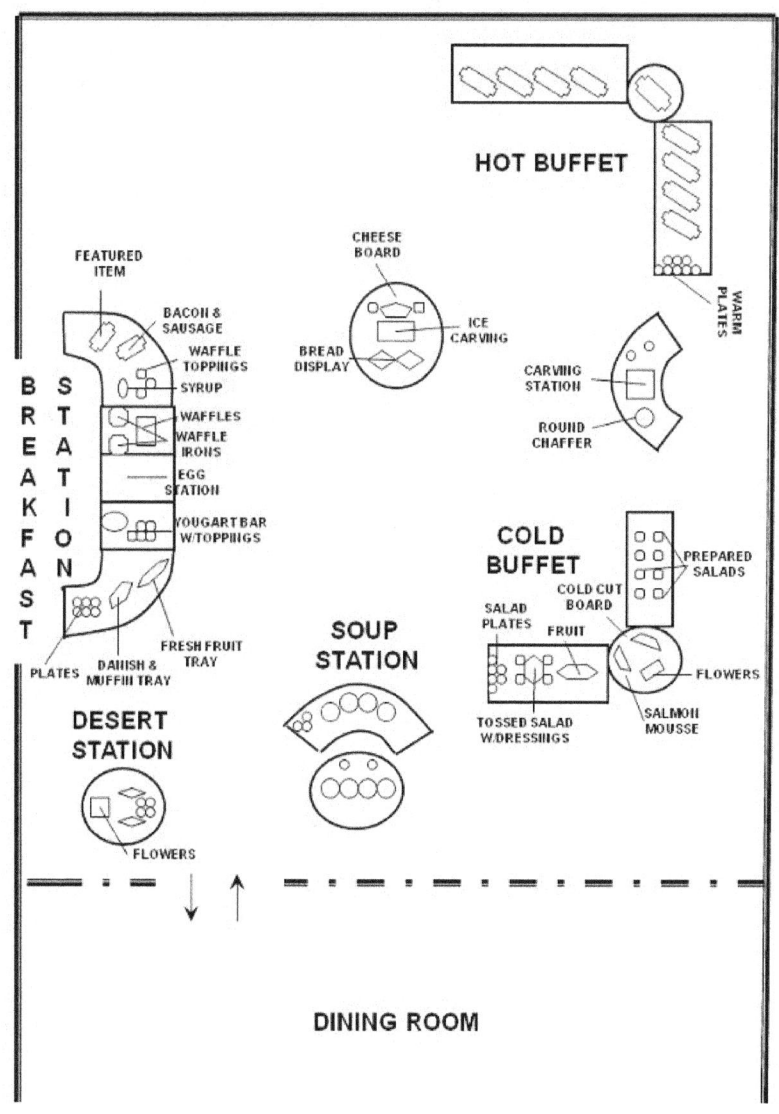

G. Service Pantries

Prior to any posted function the kitchen steward should be notified by a written set-up request sheet regarding the date and time of the function's requirements. Setups need to be ready on time to avoid the necessity of service staff having to invest time in assembling the needed supplies for the specific function. This is especially important if more than one function is scheduled. This will avoid confusion in counting and assembling the needed items, saving time and need for unnecessary extra steps to be taken.

Following a system in advance and supervised by a knowledgeable person will guarantee a smooth operation by allowing the service staff members to perform as professionals. The housekeeping department should also receive a set-up or posted request sheet regarding the placement, size, and number of tables and seats, banquet food lines and bars according to the diagram. Necessary supplies should be set prior to the all important service meetings.

To be ready:

1. Three tier carts with trays need to be assembled. These will be used for items to be used and will be placed separately on each cart shelf such as glasses, plates, and silverware. Plates and glasses do not belong on the same tray – whether setting or clearing – before being taken to the dishwashing area.
2. Set up 8 foot tables in a service area:
    a. Bread in warmer.
    b. Bus boxes for silverware.

c. Water pitchers with ice (with extra ice on the side).
d. Urns for coffee, hot water and iced tea with glasses.
e. Cocktail tray lined with a clean napkin.
f. Oval service trays lined with a clean napkin.
g. Coffee cups and saucers (if not pre-set, have extra).
h. Bread basket lined with a clean napkin.
i. Tea bags and lemons ready if requested along with tea pots.
j. Extra napkins and silverware to replace if needed.
k. Tongs for breads and extra ice in glasses, if requested.
l. Iced butter pads to replenish.
m. Cream and milk to replenish or if requested, milk.
n. Ready liners with doilies for appetizer if required as part of menu.

Proper preparation releases the server from pressure, taking unnecessary steps, and time in the event a guest requests a cup of tea. If not ready in the service area, he/she is forced to go into the kitchen and hunt for teas bags, pots and hot water. Invariably another person will decide to have tea also.

Many places are equipped with up to date service areas but it helps to be prepared and ready for any request to ensure fast and timely service. In order to be well prepared for a function – whether working alone for a party of 10 to 15 or with a partner for 20 to 30, or with a group of 20 servers for a party of 300 – the same preparation is required with the only difference being largeness. To be prepared and organized it is critical for service to be flawless. Also, avoid long conversations with guests while servicing and then only if time and other duties permit.

H. Staffing Ratio

Stand-up Cocktail Party - Two per 50 guests

Stand–up Cocktail Party with passing of Hors d'oeuvres - Two per 35 guests

Cocktails and Dinner - One per 15 guests

Dinner with Meeting (fast service) - One per 14 guests

Wedding with Bar and Toast - One per 10 guests

Gourmet or Synchronized Service - One per 8 guests

Suggestion: Banquet Coordinator should try to avoid planning hot soup of any kind as an appetizer.

I. Table Skirting

Pleating tables for banquets and special occasions is not an easy job. Pleating needs to follow a uniform standard of full skirting for all tables or even as special design.

Some establishments have purchase pleated skirting of their own design for all table sizes. Other establishments depend on pleating by their own service staff; according to a house design or as instructed otherwise bringing staff on duty one hour earlier than normally scheduled is commonly required.

Under a supervisors direction it is to make sure that all tables have pads placed properly to avoid lumps and overhanging. A proper sized tablecloth free of wrinkles, holes, and stains. Round tables must be skirted with size # 112, tablecloths set one inch above the floor with a minimum of eight pleats.

- Long 6 and 8 foot tables use 112 tablecloths.
- Round 72" tables use two sized 72 tablecloths.
- Round 60" tables use one sized 64 tablecloth.
- Round 54" tables use one sized 72 tablecloth.
- Square 30" and 36" tables use one sized 64 tablecloth.

J. Reception Requirement

For every party type, supervision of preparation, staff meetings, service supervision and consistency are vital to success. Can you imagine an opening of a Broadway show without a rehearsal? First and foremost is for the supervisor in charge to introduce themselves to the member host/hostess to insure that the function will be supervised as desired.

If host/hostess has requests or instructions:

1. Inquire about desired light setting for dinner.
2. Inquire about room temperature setting.
3. Determine the time for closing the bar or if it is to remain open during   and after dinner.
4. Determine the specific time wine is to be served or for toasting.
5. Inquire how to notify guests to sit (gong, lights, or microphone).
6. Will there be speeches?
7. Determine the time to start service and whether speed or leisure service is desired.
8. Determine if a prayer will be given.
9. No chairs are allowed to lean or rest on the table in order to secure or self-reserve a seat during the cocktail party. Suggest that an unfolded napkin on the plate will do.

First Step for a Banquet Cocktail and Dinner Reception

When the bar is closed and all guests are seated, an immediate count of empty seats should be made and immediately relayed to the chef so he can prepare accordingly. If the tables are numbered, the numbers and stands should be removed before the first course is served but allow enough time for late arrivals to find their tables.

Save Steps and Time

It is essential for one person or two, (i.e. bus person, dishwasher, or any available person) be assigned to pantry duty in order to relieve the server from the time consuming task of sorting dirty dishes and silverware. Drop and go – drop and go will allow the immediate return of the server to the table, saving steps and time, foster faster service, cause less confusion in the drop area and ensure no greasy server hands. In the event that no individual stations are assigned for any reason, it would be beneficial to have 4 servers out of 5 to clear and one of them sorting dishes in the pantry to speed clearing. Also, have ready a round tray lined with napkin containing each type of silverware for the meal in case a utensil is dropped by the guest so that it can be replaced immediately.

K. Hors d'oeuvres

The only way to good service is to concentrate on:

1) Walking erect
2) Determine the proper way to carry plates and never swing
3) Destination without guessing where to go
4) Use a facial expression that guarantees the diner's satisfaction with the food and service
5) Use a gentle manner and way to place an item on the table.
6) Use a selective tone of voice and always excuse yourself when interrupting a conversation.

There will be many times in which the perfect leisure service will be disrupted. A result of speed, short cuts (which are necessary when shorthanded), time constraints, or slow kitchen production.

Cocktail Party with Hors d'oeuvres

The server needs to arrive on time, checking the room lay-out to ensure that it is in order.

Clean white gloves a must for every Hors d'oeuvres cocktail party with an extra pair of white gloves kept in reserve.

Hors d'oeuvres

The hors d'oeuvres are passed with one hand and presented on a silver lined tray or platter while the other hand offers a cocktail napkin.

The server presents a full array of choices while a full back-up platter is ready in the pantry area that has been pre-prepared by the kitchen staff. A second staff member walks around with a lined tray to pick up or be handed empty glasses and cocktail napkins. He/she may also deliver a full new platter as a team effort.

Constant passing is essential for this type of party whether the party is for 10 or 100 guests.

L. Bar and Inventory

The bar or bars should be skirted to the floor unless portable bars are available with the back bar tables skirted to hold extra supplies. Covered tray jacks and trays for dirty glasses should be in easy to reach locations and placed in strategic positions around the room.

Unless instructed to free pour, the normal drink should be no more than 1 ½ oz. controlled pouring. Heavy pouring for a one hour cocktail party will, in many cases, result in sickness, an uncontrolled temper, difficulty in standing, and most serious of all the hazardous drive home.

Bartenders need to be inspected for cleanliness, clean and trimmed finger nails, and spotless cuffs and sleeves. While the bartender is preparing a drink, he will be observed while the drink is prepared.

The profit from liquor is basic for the all mighty bottom line. However, an inappropriate practice is to over pour for extra profit. As a result, many establishments pay a heavy price.

In any establishment and <u>by law</u> the bartender should inform management or the host that a person has had too much to drink. A bartender has the right to refuse serving an inebriated person a drink and when the bar is officially closed.

Opening and Closing Bar Preparations

The head bartender or the assistant is responsible for the proper set-up of the bar according to the specifications from the host and according to the number of guests. Requisition with appropriate inventory records are filled out to include the host's choice of liquors. The requisition also includes mixers, juices, sodas, beer, red and white wine, and American or imported sparkling wines.

Covered bus trays should be placed at the back bar containing wines, beers and sparkling wines submerged in ice. A napkin to handle is placed in front of each box.

Bare hands may not be used. All glasses must be in a straight line faced down with sparkling wine glasses face up. Glasses should be handled properly and presented with a cocktail napkin. Do not place glasses on top of one another

A hand lime or lemon squeezer should be used to squeeze the juice into the glass instead of using fingers. Use a cutting board and sharp knife for the fruit, tongs and spoons for the other garnishes.

Never scoop ice with a glass or hand from the ice bin.

Banquet Bar

Bloody Mary mix should be pre-made. If using bottled ready mix, empty it into a pitcher and serve. Do not expose ready mix bottles with labels facing the guests. All liquor labels should face the front.

Other required items include: bottle openers, cocktail shakers, cloth and cocktail napkins, mixing spoons, stirrers, tap water, strainer, juice mixers, salt, sugar and jiggers, etc. No blender is required. Try to discourage the host if they request one.

No glass racks are to be visible. No tip cups are allowed on the bar unless this is a cash bar and then only if it is permitted by management or the host. Tip cups are not recommended.

When the bar is officially closed, all bartenders are to assist in pouring sparkling wine to accommodate the toast.

Closing the Bar and Taking Inventory

All bartenders must be trained to know how to relate to portion and inventory control as well as the proper set-up of all types of bars. There are many types of bars for a host to consider according to the occasion or such factors as expense, full bar, whether for singles, type and age of guests, wine and beer only, cash bars, punch and soft drinks only, or a small portable bar.

When setting up a bar, all liquor, wine, beer, and soft drinks should be the very last items taken to the specified location of the bar.

Under any circumstance, free pouring without a pourer on each bottle is against all principles of professionalism and is a sign of disrespect to service. Proper service demands the bartender stand erect while waiting for the next guest. Avoid private conversations or jokes.

Buckets lined with bags for scraps need to be placed under the bar table. Do not hand over a beer without a glass. Keep bar neat and free of used glasses. When the scheduled time is up and permission obtained to close the bar, immediate inventory is to be taken to obtain the appropriate amount of items used when compared against the original inventory sheet of all charge back items.

Do not throw away empty bottles. The inventory is to be taken by the bar supervisor and should be done in the presence of the host or other person chosen by the host.

Empty bottles are to be counted along with the full bottles including other charge back items. The seal of a bottle of liquor is broken the host is obliged to be charged for the cost of a full bottle. The host may wish to take the opened bottles home if permitted by state law.

Another method is to charge the host by 1/10th for the amount used on each bottle. In this case the bottle stays with the establishment to be used as regular bar stock.

The rate of the original charge per bottle was agreed upon prior to the party and this is true especially for top of the shelf brands.

All charges are to be credited to liquor sales and full bottles to be returned to the stock room with the exception of used bottles transferred to the main bar counting the contents by the per tenth system and charged to the bar stock inventory. Do not leave the bar unattended after closing or at any time.

All liquor, wine, and beer are to be removed immediately after closing the bar.

All other equipment shall not to be removed during dinner and then only after all guests have departed.

Do not drink or give drinks to members of the staff.

M. Liquor Policy

(Red Alert)

The establishment will not serve alcohol to persons under the legal age under any circumstances. When in doubt, ask for a State issued I.D. that includes picture.

If the server believes a person is intoxicated, notify management immediately. If the server observes that a customer is drinking too quickly and asks for another drink, or has lost coordination, is slurring speech, is too loud, or has become obnoxious and disturbing other guests, alcohol service must cease immediately. If a server serves alcohol to an intoxicated person and that individual hurts themselves, the establishment can be held responsible as well as the individual server. By law all food and beverage service employees have the discretion and the responsibility to discontinue serving to prevent intoxicated persons from driving.

N. Bartenders and Servers

Duties: Be on time, clean and neat in appearance, and wear a name tag. Open the bar and be ready for business. Check service bar area for cleanliness, fresh ice, fruits and condiments, requisition needed supplies, glasses and water pitchers fill liquor bins with house brands and fill out appropriate inventory records.

Bartender must maintain a spotless bar top stocked with only stirrers, napkins, and compartment tray with neat assorted condiments. Use lemon and lime squeezers instead of fingers.
The free pouring of drinks at a maximum level for special members of a club or patrons of a restaurant or for the sake of a better gratuity is inappropriate and bad practice. Strong instructions need to be given to all bartenders to follow a standard pouring practice.

Just a body behind the bar does not make a bartender. It takes more than bartending knowledge and looks to be a recognized professional. Personality is a bartender's main attribute, along with friendliness and good name memory.

The bartender must be able to tolerate people with different personalities when patrons are drinking. He/she must stay alert and respect the establishment and its bylaws.

O. ABC Dinner Party Example

ABC Dinner Party requires four Servers and two Bartenders.

One Server is needed to pass canapés and assist in food service during dinner.
Three Servers are needed at 15 guests each with their own service station to rest food trays, to serve, and also assist resupplying canapés server during the cocktail party with full trays.

After the bar is officially closed, additional duties require pouring of first wine with appetizer, second wine with the main course, and serve, refill, and clear appetizer and glasses allowing the person to keep it if he/she wishes and proceed to pour the second wine before the main course arrives.

When dinner is finished, roll in the cart with after dinner cordials or by special order if requested by host.

Note: No tray jacks to be used. Serve from the service areas only.

FUNCTION PROSPECTUS

Name of Organization:___*ABC Company*___   Date Planned:_____
Will there be any promoting or any promotional material in conjunction with this party?___*No*_____
If yes, please explain: ___*n/a*_____
A.M. or P.M: ___*P.M.*_____
Function: ___*C/Dinner*_____   Date:_____   By: *SS*_____   I.P or O.P.:_____
Sponsor:_____   #:_____   Phone (O):_____   Phone (H):_____
Person Responsible for Arrangements:_____   Phone (O):_____   Phone (H):_____
Expected: *48*_____   # Guar:___*48*___   Room:_____   Price Per: *0.00*_____   +20%SC&ST
Time: Cocktails: *7:00 p.m.*   Serve: *7:45 p.m.*   Meeting: *n/a*_____   Flowers:_____

BAR:	FOOD:
	Pass: Assorted Premium Canapés
Regular Bar with Call	
BrandsAssorted Domestic and Imported Beers	------------------------------
and House Wines	
	Chilled Crabmeat Mousse "Marie Rose"
Goldfish and Pretzels on the Bar	
	Hearts of Palm Salad with Pink Peppercorns
*Roll around the After Dinner Drink Cart	
	Twin Medallions of Beef Tenderloins with Two Sauces
	Red Wine and Shallot and Mustard Hollandaise
	Seasonal Vegetables
	Chateau Potatoes
WINE:	
	Almond Basket with Fresh Berries
With Appetizer: 3300 – '88 Newton Chardonnay	
	Remarks:
With Entrée: 2730 –'80 Markham Cabernet	_____
Sauvignon	_____
	_____
	_____

SET-UP/AUDIO VISUAL INSTRUCTIONS	
6 Rounds of 8	Resupply Hors d'oeuvres:
Votive Candles on each table	_____
	_____
Bar	_____
_____	_____

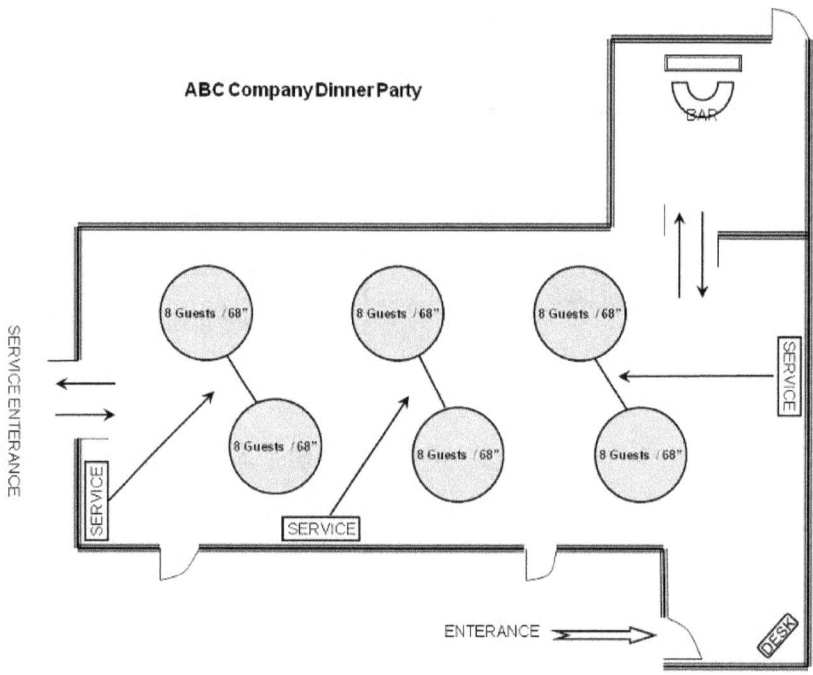

ABC Company Dinner Party

CHAPTER 10

SYNCHRONIZED SERVICE

A. White Glove Service

In the early 1980's the Cherokee Town and Country Club introduced to club membership and guests a unique way of service called "synchronized service".

The elegance of this white glove service had no equal to any other way of service, in its uniformity, timely executed, flawless, noiseless and professional service which allows an entire table of four to eight to ten persons to be served simultaneously.

Synchronized service can be one of the most elegant forms of service offered; however, it does require planning, organization, coordination and most importantly, attention to detail.

With the correct combination of these techniques, the staff needs to follow and be prepared to offer the finest level of service from private clubs to upgraded restaurants and major hotels. Teaching servers is a skill taught by talented supervisors who can do almost anything.

B. Team Selection

Begin dry runs according to the menu to be served. The food and beverage servers should consist of four servers per station of three tables of eight persons each. In addition four bar personnel are required to complete the service crew.

First establish three groups of four along with four beverage servers (one per station and one floater). Choose a leader for each team as the number one server followed by teammates two, three and four and one, two, three for beverage servers.

C. Service Area

The food will be pre-plated in the kitchen and placed in hot carts and lined by the kitchen staff and will be ready for the teams of four to pick-up two plates each from each of the two service areas. A line will be formed by the supervisor for entrance to the room. The supervisor will signal for the team to follow, in line, the team leader and teammates will go to their specific table locations.

When all are in their designated places the leader will nod his head as a signal to begin serving. While carrying two plates each, start from the first person to his/her right to serve with the left hand by placing the plate 2" from the rim of the table and placing the main entrée facing the person switching the plate from the right hand to the left and then serve the next person to their left the same way. Note: After all persons are served, the leader will peel off first toward the exit, in unison, followed by the number two and three servers with the fourth waiting to exit behind number three.

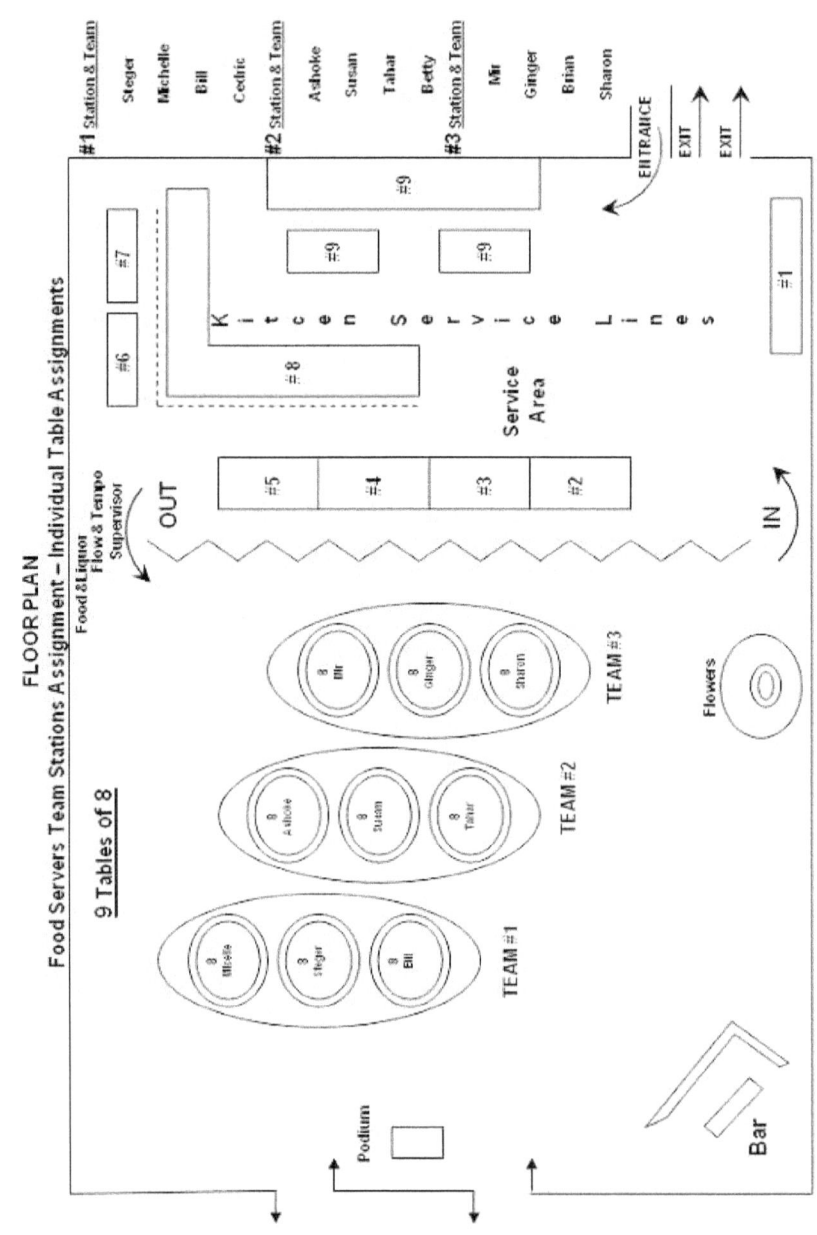

FLOOR PLAN
Food Servers Team Stations Assignment – Individual Table Assignments

#1 Station & Team
Steger
Michelle
Bill
Cedric

#2 Station & Team
Ashoke
Susan
Tahar
Betty

#3 Station & Team
Mr
Ginger
Brian
Sharon

ENTRANCE
EXIT
EXIT

9 Tables of 8

Food & Liquor
Flow & Tempo
Supervisor

OUT

IN

Kitchen Service Lines

Service Area

#9
#9
#9

#6
#7
#8

#5
#4
#3
#2

#1

TEAM #1
8 Michelle
8 Steger
8 Bill

TEAM #2
8 Ashoke
8 Susan
8 Tahar

TEAM #3
8 Mr
8 Ginger
8 Sharon

Flowers

Podium

Bar

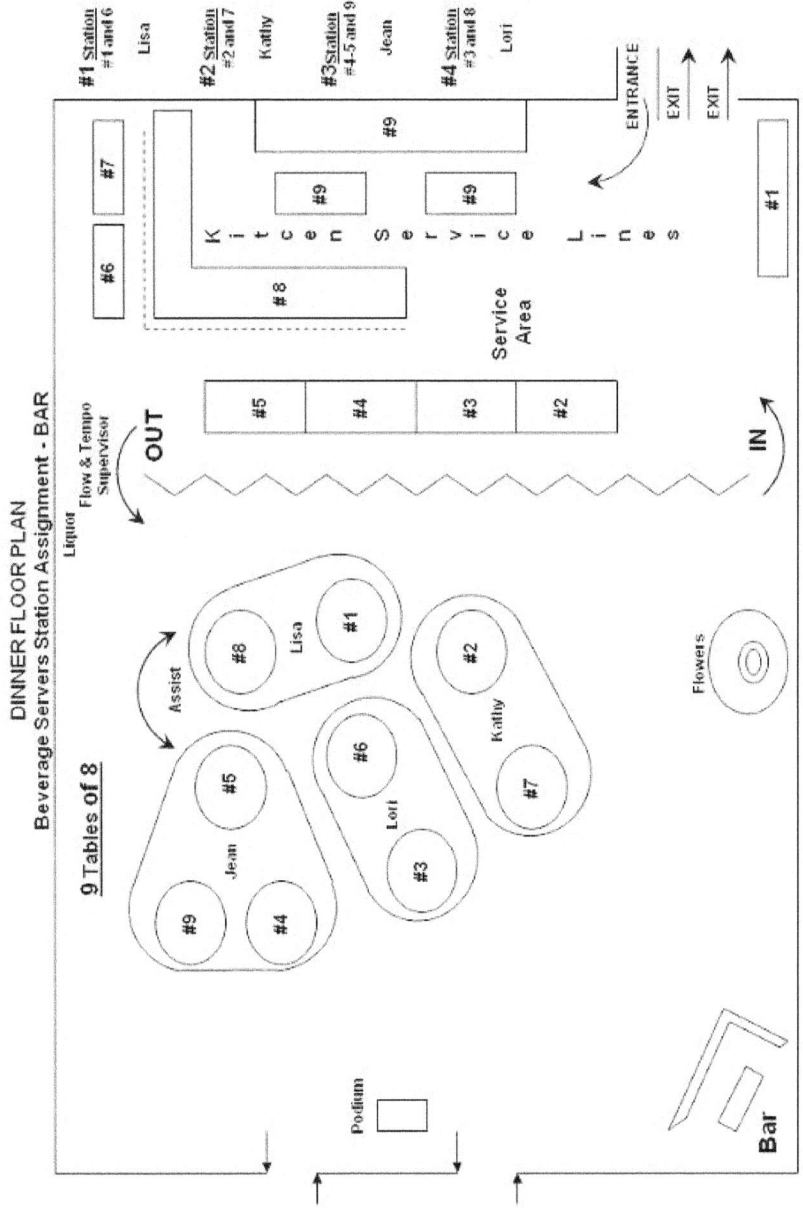

DINNER FLOOR PLAN
Beverage Servers Station Assignment - BAR

Practice – Practice

Many dry runs are required before the actual event to eliminate mistakes in executing the perfect flow of service.

The same system is applied in clearing as in service with the only exception being that the server will start clearing with the person to their left instead of right and after clearing wait until the entire table is cleared before the leader begins to peel off .

After the course is served the leader of each team will assign two teammates to circulate around a table. This to ensure that service between courses, i.e. pouring water, passing bread, butter or other various items, is attended to throughout the entire service until the very end.

D. Beverage Service

Beverage service is handled in the same manner. However, the guest to service ratio should be fifteen to one person. Although the food and beverage service teams work independently of one another, having dry runs together at the beginning is a must. The key to any form of food service is the organization of all tasks and responsibilities related to all aspects of the menu and service.

E. Set Up and Floor Plan

First Step

The first step is to organize the necessary utensils and items required for each course to be served. It is best to write the requirements to clearly communicate them to the necessary personnel to provide efficient access for room set-up and service.

Each utensil is assigned to a specific place and organized with the menu and method of service as the direction of service is indicated which allows both smooth transfer patterns; avoiding a crossing of traffic and confusion.

Food & Liquor Floor Plan

F. Flow and Tempo

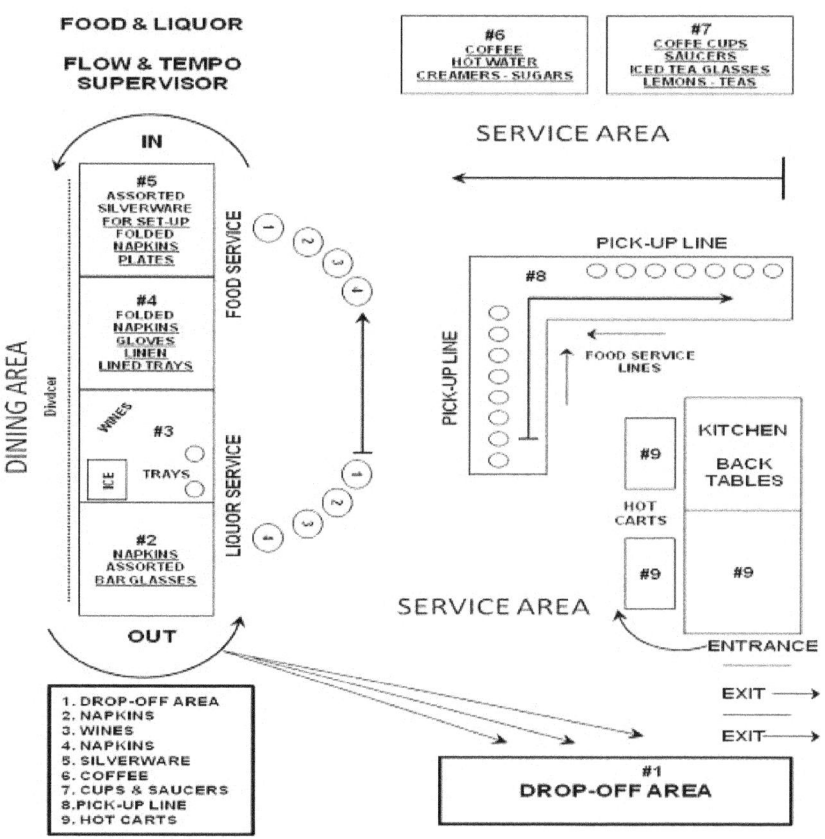

Second Step

The second step is to clearly outline how each place setting is to be arranged. This provides consistency and uniformity of each place setting throughout the room per the first setting.

The next step in synchronized service is the organization to service itself. This begins by outlining the order and method of servicing and clearing.

This document illustrates specific detail and movement in which service is to be executed. It also serves as the script for the supervisor to orchestrate the service for the entire function.

The supervisor will direct and instruct the servers waiting to enter the room and will also ensure that the service flows smoothly so as to appear unobtrusive to guests.

This can be accomplished by placing the teams with ten second intervals as they enter the room and go to a specific table. To further ensure a smooth flowing service each server is assigned to two specific seat numbers for serving and clearing each table as illustrated. The specific direction as indicated by arrows for entering and exiting each table is conducted in one harmonious file.

Once all the servers are in place each server relies upon the leader's eye contact for the signal to present or clear a course. Remember two important areas in service: present and clear each course with the server's palm of their hand always toward the guest and in clearing. Never cross the guest by picking up the forks from the right.

This synchronized service provides inspiration for the guests. Guests will be impressed by the team work as it achieves the expectations of the establishment and demonstrates the staff's professional abilities.

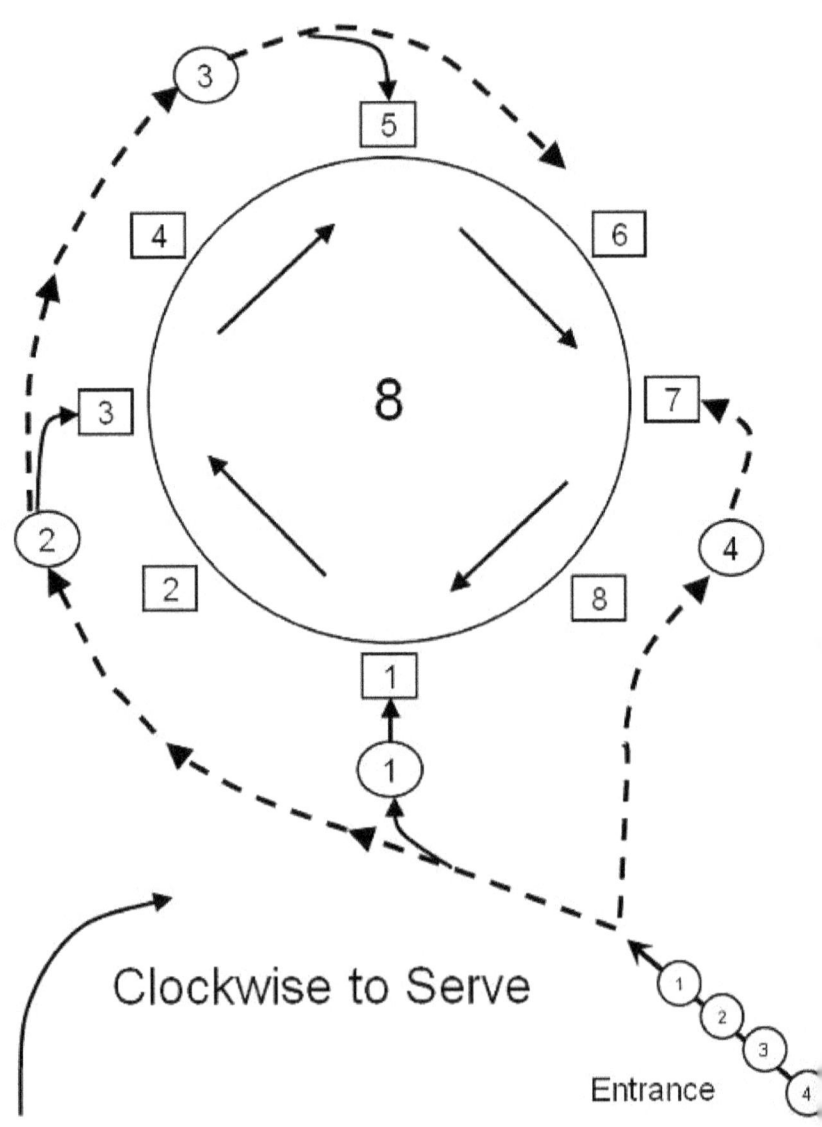

Clockwise to Serve

Entrance

Counter-Clockwise for Clearing

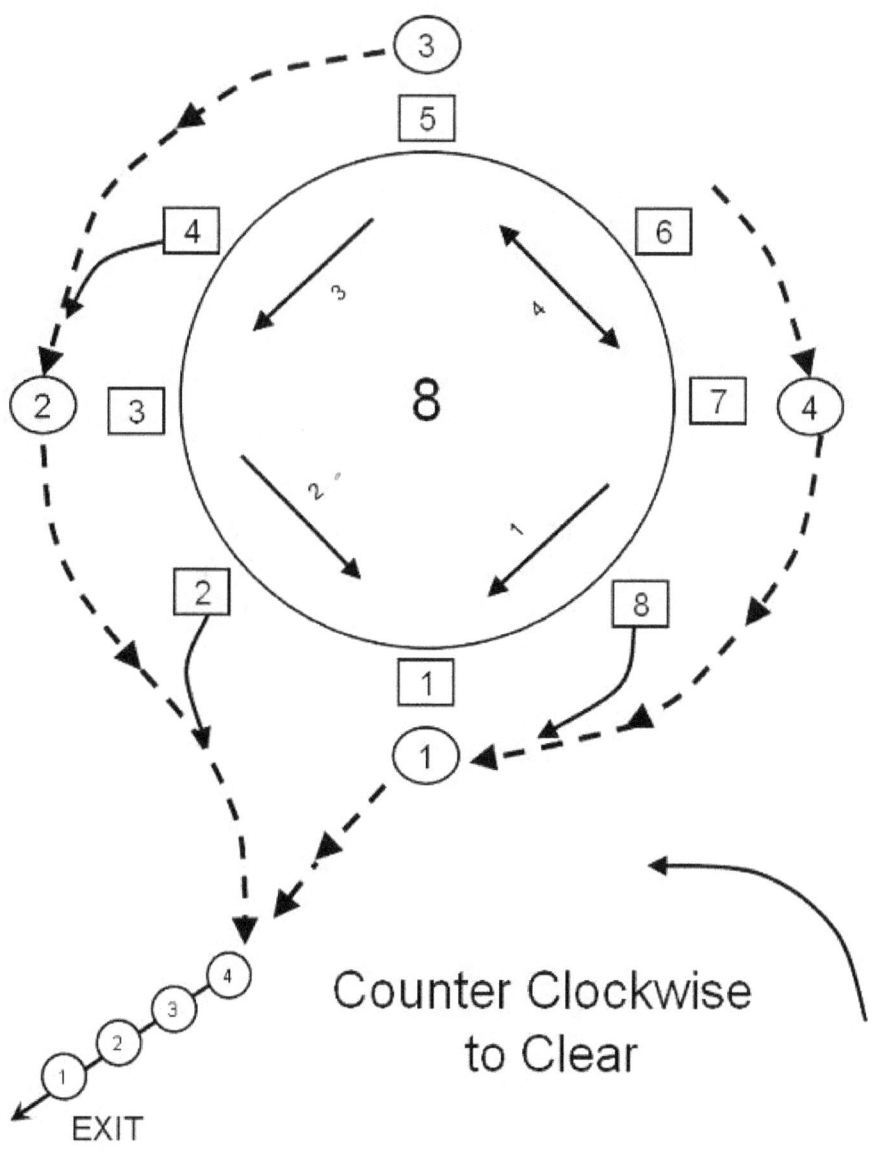

Third Step

When all the necessary duties are done and the room and dining areas are staged and checked by the supervisor, the room now is open as scheduled on time.

As a recommendation and with the host's approval, a line is to be formed by eight servers four on each side of the entrance to silently welcome the arriving guests with a simple smile.

If there is a cocktail hour, and when it is over, and when the guests are seated, the team leaders will pick-up the numbered table stands from their individually assigned tables. However, do not rush; allowing for late arrivals.

At this time the two servers assigned by each team will pour water into iced goblets at once but not lifting the glass off the table to pour. The beverage servers will pour the first glass half full of chosen wine not lifting the glass off the table, being careful that the neck of the bottle does not touch the glass. Ladies are served first.

If no speeches are scheduled, food service will now start with the first team of four servers entering the room holding two plates each to serve. The supervisor will allow ten seconds before the second team of four will enter then follow with the third team and fourth team using the same technique throughout the meal.

Service Area and Service

Following the service technique as noted on the two pick-up lines, courses will be lined in two pick-up lines in the service area for immediate pick-up lined by the entrance and given the cue by the supervisor to enter and serve.

The kitchen staff will be readying to place the next course for pick-up after the first course is cleared and the beverage staff pours the wine.

The supervisor orchestrating the service will not move from their post at any time and will scout the dining room and service area making sure that the service area remains in perfect order. He/she is the orchestration leader from start to finish.

When the time is ready for clearing, the supervisor makes absolutely sure every station's tables have finished the course which is sometimes delayed due to slow eaters. They then proceed and start clearing from the right to left and then pull out in unison.

After each course is served only the two servers from each team will circulate every five minutes through the dinner to observe any needed items. Servers are not to be standing at anytime in one place; moving at the supervisor's direction to do so. All teams will stand by the service area awaiting the next direction to perform.

When the last course is served and cleared all servers should be out of the dining room unless directed otherwise by the supervisor. This is particularly true if speeches or presentations are in progress. Only one person per team is allowed to pour more coffee or water if desired until the end of the function and the last guest has departed. Guests may return to their table to finish their drink.

If the bar is to be reopened, no tables are to be cleared until the end of the function and after the last guest has departed.

This type of service is not new but is practiced only by five star hotels and upgrade establishments which have ample room available. Synchronized service requires knowledgeable directors, managers and supervisors who depend on their ability to perform this type of service. A club, hotel or any establishment can do the same by learning and adopting this complicated, yet simple way of service which requires careful training.

The purpose of this service is to enhance the reputation of the establishment. No establishment regardless of the number of its members, customers, location and pricing should ignore that after love of good food comes how a patron feels they were treated.

General

The service area can be assembled in other areas if a divider is not available to separate the service area from the dining room. It can be set in an adjoining room, existing service room area or directly from the main kitchen to table if near the function.

The service area should be designed according to menu, location, number of persons, number of courses and the distance between the pick-up line and the destination. If the service area is near the dining room there is no need for the plates to be covered but all plates should be covered to maintain temperature of the plated foods. Servers must not swing their arms when carrying plates or any other item and must keep elbows to the body's side.

Voice and noise from the service areas must be held to a very minimum - especially in the service pick-up areas and in the return drop-off areas. This requires special attention for the sound and noise caused from dropping plates is most unprofessional and disturbing to guests.

It is now appropriate for the supervisor and management to hold a short meeting of all involved to thank them for their outstanding service.

G. The Industry

There is an ending to everything including one for this book.

Appendix

CLASSIC AFFINITIES OF WINE AND FOOD

Revised 10/2010
Compiled by Lisa Taylor and John Jordan

White Wines: Dry, Light bodied Whites

Wine

Sherry
Beaujolais Blanc
Italian Chardonnay
Frascati
Macon-Villages
Muscadet
Orvieto

Pinot Grigio
Riesling, Kabinett
Sauvingnon Blanc
Soave
Trebbiano
Verdicchio
Vinho Verdi

Dry, Medium-bodied Whites

Albarino
Bavi ST. Veran
Graves (White)
Pinot Grigio
Poulilly Fuisse
Pouilly Fume

Riesling (Alsace)
Sancerre
Sylvaner (Alsace)

Off-Dry, Medium-bodied Whites (A touch of sweetness)

Chardonnay (France)

Riesling

Chenin Blanc
French Colombard
Gewurztraminer
Pinot Noir Blanc

Semillon
Soave
White Zinfandel
Verdicchio
Vouvray (Demi-sec)

Full-bodied, Complex Flavor Wines

Chablis
Chardonnay (California)
Chassagne-Montrachet
Corton-Charlemagne

Hermitage Blanc
Marsanne, Roussane
Meursault
Montrachet
Puligny Montrachet
Viognier

Asti Spumante
Eiswein
Gewurztraminer
(Late Harvest)
Muscato

Riesling (Late Harvest)
Riesling (Auslese
Beerenauslese,
Trockenbeerenauslese)
Sauternes

Red Wines

Light and Fruity

Bardolino
Beaujolais
Brouilly
Cabernet Franc
Chiroubles
Cotes De Beaune-Villages

Cotes Du Rhone
Dolcetto
Gamay
Lambrusco
Napa Gamay
Tannat
Valipolicella
All Nouveau Style
Reds

Medium-bodied

Barbera
Chianti
Pinotage
Pinot Noir
Rioja

Rich, Classic, Full-bodied

Barbaresco
Beaune
Bordeaux
Cabernet Sauvignon
Chambolle Musigny
Clos Du Tart
Corton
Cote-Rotie
Echezeaux
Fixin
Gevrey Chambertin

La Romanee
Malbec (Young)
Merlot
Morey-Saint-Denis
Nuitis-St. George
Pommard
Syrah
Montepulciano
Volnay
Vosne Romanee

Robust, Very Full-bodied

Amarone
Barolo
Brunello Di Montalcino
Chambertin
Charbono
Chateauneuf-Du-Pape
Clos Vougeot
Cornas

Cote Rotie
Gigondas
Hemitage
La Tache
Malbec (Older & Reserve)
Petite Sirah
Richebourg
Shiraz

Charbono   Zinfandel
Chateauneuf-Du-Pape
Clos Vougeot
Cornas

Desert Reds

Madeira
Marsala
Mavrodaphne
Sherry
Vintage Ports
Late-Harvest Zinfandel

Food with Tawny Port

10-year old tawnies with: salted roasted almonds; chicken
or duck liver parfait or other meaty pates and terrines;
 presunto (Portuguese air-dried ham); pecans, almond
or walnut tart; apple, pear or banana tatin; a compote of
 dried fruits; crèam brûlée; cheesecake (without red fruits);
 ginger-flavored cakes and puddings
20-year old tawnies with: foie gras – an alternative to
Sauternes, roast lobster (according to Calem), game
such as pheasant and partridge, hard sheep's milk
cheeses, mature Gouda, Parmesan, dark chocolate or
chocolate truffles, biscotti, panforte di Siena, roasted
chestnuts

Wines & Grape Varietals

Whites

Chardonnay

USED IN: Burgundy, Chablis, and most Blanc de Blancs Champagnes and sparkling wines

Chenin Blanc

USED IN: Vouvray (Loire), Steen (SouthAfrica). Sweet versions include Coteaux du Layon, Bonnezeaux, and Quarts de Chaume.

Sauvignon Blanc

USED IN: Sancerre, Pouilly-Fumé, Fumé Blanc (in California and Washington)

Reds

Cabernet Sauvignon

USED IN: Bordeaux from the Médoc, including St.-Estèphe, St.-Julien, Margaux and Pauillac (often blended with Merlot)

Gamay

USED IN: Beaujolais Nouveauk Beaujolais-Villages, Brouilly, Fleurie, Morgon, Julienas, Moulin-à-Vent and other Beaujolais crus

Grenache / Garnacha

USED IN: Chateauneuf-du-Pape, Priorat (Spain)

Merlot

USED IN: Pomerol and Saint-Emilion, often blended with Cabernet Sauvignon and/or Cabernet Franc

Nebbiolo	USED IN: Barbaresco, Barolo, Gattinara (Piedmont, Italy)
Pinot Noir	USED IN: Various Burgundy appellations
Sangiovese	USED IN: Chianti, Brunello di Montalcino, Vino Nobile di Montepulciano (Tuscany,Italy)
Syrah / Shiraz	USED IN: Hermitage, Côte-Rôtie, Cornas,Crozes-Hermitage
Tempranillo / Tinta Roriz	USED IN: Rioja, Ribera del duero (Spain);various wines from Portugal

Generally Speaking

The fattier the fish or the heavier the sauce; the fuller bodied, more assertive and fruitier the wine.

Wine is not customary with salads.

Beef depending on the method of cooking, sauce, seasoning and cut of meat; the finer the cut, the finer the wine.

Buy wine over apples, sell wine over cheese. Stronger cheeses need more robust and assertive wines.

Large bottles mature more slowly than small ones.

Time Tested Affinities

Brut champagne with caviar
Sparkling wines as aperitifs
Red Bordeaux from the Médoc with "fine" game
Red Cote De Nuits Burgundy with prime roast beef
French Sauternes with ripe peach
Vintage Port with a mature stilton
Chablis with plump oysters
White Montrachet or Meursault with delicate flavored or fine textured butter-sauced fish, such as tubot or sole
Chilled Rose or white Zinfandel with a picnic lunch
California Zinfandel with Thanksgiving turkey
Fine Cabernet Sauvignon or Bordeaux with lamb
Sherry with consummé
Sauternes with Roquefort cheese (this is the only wine which will fare well with Roquefort), but sweet wines will go well with other bleu cheeses as well
Alsatian Riesling with sausage dishes
Dry Gewurztraminer with duck liver pate
Sauternes with foie gras

Pomerol with black truffles
Big, fruit intense Shirazes are great with red meats slathered in barbeque sauce

Contrasting Flavors

Although they do not have similar flavors, many foods and wines may have a flavor affinity for a contrasting flavor and the resulting combination my enhance each when served together.
Chardonnay: Orange, tarragon, pistachios
Fumé Blanc: Red bell peppers, marjoram, mustard
Dry Chenin Blanc: Capers, dill, almonds
Colombard: Mint, fennel, cashews
Grenache: Curry, orange, mint, cinnamon
Cabernet: Nutmeg, thyme, wild rice, pecans
Syrah: Rosemary, cinnamon, tomatoes
Zinfandel: Caraway, tomatoes, sage, mustard

Foods That Fight Wines

Vinegar and condiments that contain it; like mustards, pickles, salad dressings and relishes make wine taste flat.
Very spicy foods, particularly those containing hot spices like chilies or peppercorns, can overwhelm all but the staunchest wines. Beer is often a better choice with such foods.
Salty foods can prove difficult with most wines although champagne cuts through the intensity very well.
Other foods that kill the taste of wine are: anchovies, citrus (particularly grapefruit), mayonnaise, chocolate, sweets that are intensely syrupy or sugary, avocados,

pineapple, bananas candied vegetables, egg yolks, cranberries, molasses, tomatoes, onions, garlic, coffee and to a much lesser degree tea.

Over ripened brie or gorgonzola.

Vegetable acids compete with wine. Vegetables, such as artichokes, asparagus, spinach and sorrel are high in acid which can diminish the pleasures of wine. Try using sweet spices or sauces containing cheese, cream, mayonnaise or other dairy products to minimize the competitive effect. Grilling, frying, or serving them raw in salads with olive oil or lemon also helps to mitigate the competing acids.

Non-Food Items That Are Enemies of Wine

Tobacco smoke – particularly that which is from pipes and cigars.

The common cold, hay feer and bronchial asthma.

Heavy perfume.

Other Possibilities to Consider

Oysters with an oaked white Bordeaux

Shellfish cocktail - chilled dry rose or even a pink Spanish Cava

Prawns with a Verdelho

Lobster Thermidor – aged red Burgundy

White truffles – Barolo and Barbaresco

Though difficult to overcome the palate coating effect of very rich, dark, sweet, molten chocolate; try as sweet red such as Recioto della Valpolicella, Vintage Port, Orange Muscat, or even some Cabernet Souvignons

Meaty fish such as black seabass, turbot, monkfish, dover sole – woody Chardonnay, heavier Beaujolais, Pinot Noir, Syrah, Merlot, Zinfandel

Mild fish such as grouper flounder, sole, and skate –
Chardonnay and Chablis
Shrimp and raw oysters – Champagne and Sparkling
wines
Confit of Duck – Tannat
Green and yellow tomatoes – Crisp white
Golden and orange tomatoes – Richer, rounder whites

Dark tomatoes – full bodied reds but avoid oaky or
tannic wines
Grilled or baked tomatoes – spicy red wine
Buffalo – Cabernet Sauvignon, Bordeaux blends and
Brunello
Yak – Pinot Meunier and Cabernet Sauvignon in
general, and is an excellent fit with Chilean Cabernet
blend Almaviva (Almavivia is a blend of Cabernet
Sauvignon, Carmenere and Cabernet Franc)
Ostrich – the slightly gamy flavor is nicely off-set by
the forward fruit of Shiraz
Venison – an excellent match to the spicy tannins of
Malbec and Malbec blends
Elk – pairs well with the acidity of Pinot Meunier and
Pinot Noir
Pheasant – Pheasant can easily stand up to a red, the
crispness of white compliments its rich denseness. Un-
oaked Chardonnay, Viognier and Colombard all work
well. Can also pair well with Rose Champagnes.

For Wine with Vegetarian Dishes
To match rich whites, add:

Rich unctuous purées enriched with cream and/or
butter
Vegetable gratins with crispy toppings

Nuts (especially almonds and hazelnuts). They pick up on the flavor of oak, especially oaked whites.
Roasted pine nuts or pumpkin seeds
Pulses such as lentils and coco beans
A little cream to vinaigrettes
Sweet, rich vegetable such as sweet potato, butternut squash and roast red peppers

To match medium-full-bodies reds:

Add warm spices such as cinnamon, ginger and five spice (though use the latter in moderation)
Enhance flavor by roasting, grilling and barbecuing

To match medium-full-bodied reds

Use miso or soy sauce (even Marmite) in sauces to replicate meaty flavors
Drizzle aged balsamic vinegar over your food
Add shaved cheeses such as Parmesan and Asagio
Add mushroom, especially porcini and chestnuts

Final Thoughts
How Many Grapes Does it Take?
1 grape cluster = 1 glass
75 grapes = 1 cluster
4 clusters = 1 bottle
40 clusters = 1 vine
1 vine = 10 bottles
1200 clusters – 1 barrel
1 barrel = 60 gallons
60 gallons = 25 cases
30 vines = 1 barrel
400 vines = 1 acre
1 acre = 5 tons
5 tons = 332 acres

Bottle Sizes

Bottles	Litres	Bordeaux Rhone	Champagne/Burgundy/New World	California
.05′	0.375	Half Bottle/Split/Pony	Half Bottle/Split/Pony	Half Bottle/Split/Pony
1	0.75	Bottle	Bottle	Bottle
2	1.50	Magnum	Magnum	Magnum
3	2.25	Marie-Jean	N/A	N/A
4	3.00	Double Magnum	Jeroboam	Double Magnum
6	4.50	Jeroboam	Rehoboam	N/A
6.67	5.0	N/A	N/A	Jeroboam

	0			
8	6.00	Imperial Magnum	Methuselah	Imperial
12	9.00	N/A	Salmanazar	Salmanazar
16	12.00	Balthazar	Balthazar	Balthazar
20	15.00	Nebuchadnezzar	Nebuchadnezzar	Nebuchadnezzar
24	18.00	Melchior	Melchior	Melchior
34	25.50	Sovereign	Sovereign	Sovereign